Change
Is
EVERYBODY'S
Business

$$\frac{2\times(11/07)}{11/10}$$

$$2\times \; {}^{11}\!/_{07} - {}^{4}\!/_{08}$$

2002
4×12/10 a/.11

Change
Is
EVERYBODY'S
Business

PAT McLAGAN

Artwork by Jonathan Davis
Johannesburg, South Africa

BK

BERRETT-KOEHLER PUBLISHERS, INC.
San Francisco

Berrett-Koehler Publishers, Inc.
235 Montgomery Street, Suite 650
San Francisco, CA 94104-2916
Tel: (415) 288-0260
Fax: (415) 362-2512
www.bkconnection.com

Ordering Information
Quantity sales. Special discounts are available on quantity purchases by corporations, associations, and others. For details, contact the "Special Sales Department" at the Berrett-Koehler address above.
Individual sales. Berrett-Koehler publications are available through most bookstores. They can also be ordered direct from Berrett-Koehler: Tel: (800) 929-2929; Fax: (802) 864-7626; www.bkconnection.com
Orders for college textbook/course adoption use. Please contact Berrett-Koehler: Tel: (800) 929-2929; Fax: (802) 864-7626.
Orders by U.S. trade bookstores and wholesalers. Please contact Publishers Group West, 1700 Fourth Street, Berkeley, CA 94710. Tel: (510) 528-1444; Fax (510) 528-3444.

Berrett-Koehler and the BK logo are registered trademarks
of Berrett-Koehler Publishers, Inc.

Printed in the United States of America

Berrett-Koehler books are printed on long-lasting acid-free paper. When it is available, we choose paper that has been manufactured by environmentally responsible processes. These may include using trees grown in sustainable forests, incorporating recycled paper, minimizing chlorine in bleaching, or recycling the energy produced at the paper mill.

Library of Congress Cataloging-in-Publication Data

McLagan, Parricia A.
    Change is everybody's business : claim your change power / Pat McLagan.
        p.   cm.
    Includes bibliographical references and index.
    ISBN 1–57675–190–2
    1. Organizational change—Handbooks, manuals, etc.   2. Self-actualization (Psychology)—Handbooks, manuals, etc.   3. Job satisfaction—Handbooks, manuals, etc.   I. Title.
HD58.8.M348 2002   658.4'06—dc21
                                                                          2002023229

07 06 05 04 03 02   10 9 8 7 6 5 4 3 2 1

Interior Design & Typesetting by Desktop Miracles, Inc., Stowe, Vermont

Dedicated to my Mom and Dad, who lived through the turmoil and promise of the 20th century and almost saw its passing.

Bernice Moldenhauer (1919–1996)
Harry Moldenhauer (1904–1996)

THANKS for being transition people, for bringing me into this fascinating and changing world, and for encouraging me to make my mark in it!!

Contents

An important note from the author to you **ix**

Acknowledgments **xi**

Foreword **xiii**

Introduction: Claim Your Change Power **1**

Part I: Powerful Beliefs

Belief #1: What is "Normal" **9**

Belief #2: On Resistance and Negative Emotions **13**

Belief #3: When Change Starts **19**

Belief #4: How Deliberate Change Happens **25**

Belief #5: When to Commit **29**

Belief #6: The Role of Formal Leaders **33**

Belief #7: The Role of Followers **39**

Part I Conclusion **45**

What is Your Empowering Belief Quotient? **47**

Part II: Powerful Character

Character Lesson #1: Stand for Something **59**

Character Lesson #2: Be Aware of Your
Beliefs and Assumptions **63**

Character Lesson #3: Use Your Emotions **69**

Character Lesson #4: Add Value in Your World **75**

Part II Conclusion **81**

How Empowering is Your Character? A Questionnaire **83**

Part III: Powerful Actions

Action Lesson #1: Be a Business   89

Action Lesson #2: Develop Information Age Skills   95

Action Lesson #3: Be Your Own Human
Resource Manager   101

Action Lesson #4: Take Charge of Your Own
Change Process   111

Part III Conclusion   119

How Empowered are Your Actions? A Questionnaire   121

Afterword   125

Resources and Background: A Special Bibliography   127

Index   133

An important note from the author to you

HAVE YOU EVER eaten an energy bar? It helps you bring your own power and resources to the surface. *Change Is EVERYBODY's Business* is meant to be an energy bar for you in working with change. I'm writing it because in over 30 years of consulting all over the world, I've seen few people fully access their change power. Instead, I've seen disillusionment, fear, blaming, "stuckness," and dependency. I want it better for us.

I want both of us, all of us, to claim our change power—unleash it in ways that help us create a better personal and shared world. It's something you and we CAN do. The question is, "WILL we?"

Whatever role you play at work or at home, you are a force in change. Mail clerk or CEO, salesperson or factory worker, leader or follower, wife or husband, old or young—you are an active participant in the changes around you. And you have choices in the roles you'll play. You can choose how you *think about* what's happening around you. And you can choose your *actions*. These choices are the heart of "empowerment." And empowerment is a gift we give ourselves, not something that others bestow.

Change Is EVERYBODY's Business is about personal empowerment—from the inside out. It focuses on personal power at work, but it is relevant to all areas of life. Chances are that by developing your change power at work, you will become more powerful wherever you go.

My role in this book is to remind you about what you already know but may not be fully acting on. It is to remind you that your actions or indifference help to create the world as we know it. That's your *external* impact. Your thoughts also create the world as YOU know it—your *inner* world. This is a lot of *power*. I'd like to help you learn or ascertain how to access and use that power.

I hope you will find many interesting, provocative, and awakening messages in *Change Is EVERYBODY's Business* to help you navigate the churning waters that change inevitably causes. That's my mission. Let me know what happens for you.

Pat McLagan

patmclagan@mclaganinternational.com

Acknowledgments

Many thanks to several dear friends and colleagues who carefully read and helped me shape *Change Is EVERYBODY's Business*:

Boyce Appel	Kevin O'Sullivan
Frank Basler	Deb Santagata
Geoff Bellman	Bob Stump
Peggy Hutcheson	Mavis Wilson
Nancy Kuhn	Richard Whiteley
Michael Mitch	Chrystie Hill

I'm grateful for your support and friendship!

Foreword

BY KENNETH BLANCHARD, PH.D
Co-Author, *The One Minute Manager®*

Change is a topic we never seem to learn enough about. The phenomenal success of *Who Moved My Cheese*, whose Foreword I also wrote, is evidence to that. We feel exhilarated, yes, but also overwhelmed and out of control in a world that continually moves our cheese. We need to rethink our roles and reactions.

This book picks up where *Who Moved My Cheese* left off. It distills a wealth of knowledge and practice. It is readable and a kind of "field guide" for dealing with change, whoever and wherever you are. The bottom line is that, with the help of insights and tips in this book, you can mine and *claim your change power.* It's in your reach—in *everybody's* reach.

There are many books out there on empowerment and change, including my own, *Empowerment Takes More Than a Minute.* In this field, *Change Is Everybody's Business* has a special place. It expresses many profound ideas, but in a simple and approachable way. It is brief, but presents important and broad perspectives. It is practical, but clearly grounded in a wise and deep understanding of people at work, people in change.

Specifically, *Change Is Everybody's Business* makes it clear that our beliefs, character and actions create us and our world of work. And, it shows us how to be powerful players in shifting sands, whatever our job, whatever our formal authority.

Pat McLagan has been influential in the change management field for years, working on change in executive meeting rooms and in the trenches. She's hung in there with management boards, leadership groups, change facilitators, and the people themselves—as they struggled with new directions and challenges. She's supported change in just about every kind of organization, numerous industries, with all kinds of people, and in many countries—including South Africa before, during and after the end of apartheid.

So, what she writes about here isn't the latest catchy idea. It's grounded in gritty experience and a lifetime of paying attention to how change happens in people and at work. In this simple and short book, she distills a wealth of knowledge and experience, making it fresh and accessible to all of us for action.

For example, it's refreshing to recognize that resistance is a wake-up call rather than a problem to avoid . . . that leaders need to be committed learners rather than having to put up a front of perfection . . . that we can use rather than deny emotions. We can act as though each of us is a business within the larger business. And, as she says in Action Lesson #3, ". . . put yourself in the driver's seat. Don't hand your management of yourself over to anyone—not to human resources, not to management—not to anyone else." This isn't a call to mayhem. It's a call to responsible and conscious use of power.

It's in both our and our organizations' best interests to respond to this call to claim our change power—to make change *everybody's* business. Enjoy!!

> *Ken Blanchard*
> *San Diego, California*

Claim Your Change Power

Change Is EVERYBODY's Business is about your change power at and around work. But you can't really separate your life and work. You've got to focus on both in order to make change your friend. To make it something you revel in and walk into, rather than away from.

This book will help you develop the point of view and the practices for thriving in change. It will help you see its important role in your life and work. You'll be better able to influence its impact on you and on the people you work with and for. *Change Is EVERYBODY'S Business* does the following:

Part 1: <u>**Powerful Beliefs.**</u> Your beliefs drive many of your actions. They also help shape how you view the world around you. You'll examine seven important belief areas, make your own current beliefs more conscious, and commit to beliefs that will best shape your future.

Part 2: <u>**Powerful Character.**</u> Who you ARE is a major part of your impact—of your power. This is why we all agree, "actions speak louder than words." This section describes four key character traits that support personal effectiveness in change.

Part 3: <u>**Powerful Actions.**</u> The actions you ultimately take are a combination of your beliefs, your character, and your capacity for action. In this section you'll be challenged to develop the capacity for action that will help you be successful as a player in these more open and participative times.

You can read one, two or all three parts, and read them in any order. Follow your needs and interests. You have the power!

There is a self-assessment questionnaire at the end of each section. I think you will get more benefit if you take the questionnaires *before* you read each section. It's up to you.

This is a very personal book. I will talk with you as a colleague, a co-learner, and a fellow 21st century citizen. Change is my main interest in life, and I am excited to share what I have learned with you.

It will help if you take a few minutes to anchor yourself in the topic. So, before you read on, take some time to think about the changes that you have faced in your recent past—even face right now.

What is changing around you—and personally affecting you— that you feel you have *absolutely no control over?* (It could be a death, a law that is changing how your organization must work, a downsizing decision, or new technology.)

What is changing around you—and personally affecting you— that is someone else's decision, but is *something you can still*

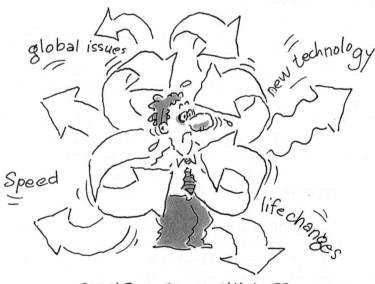

FACING LOTS OF CHANGES

influence? (Like a shift in allocation of work, decisions about how your team will work together, etc.)

What changes are you experiencing in your life due to just getting older and moving to a *different stage in your life?* (Like a child moving out, dealing with weight problems, or feeling a need to use important skills and pursue interests you put aside years ago.)

What changes are you *trying to make happen—initiating?*

What other changes are coming into your life—from *any source?*

The answers to these questions will help you personalize your insights as you read and think about what follows. Enjoy your journey!!

PART I

Powerful Beliefs

YOUR BELIEFS ABOUT CHANGE have a lot of impact on what you do. Therefore, *beliefs are often more important in change than techniques.* Techniques work when you *think* to use them. They operate situation by situation. Beliefs, on the other hand, influence your entire life and choices—what you see and don't see. They affect whether you even think to or want to use "techniques."

Stan, a team leader, knew three great techniques for negotiating with people who disagreed with him. But he believed that people

BELIEFS VS. TECHNIQUES

should obey authority. So even though he knew the techniques, he *didn't recognize* many situations where he could use them.

A Recent History of Beliefs

Science in the latter part of the 1900s transformed our view of the world. Since the 17th century, OUR *belief* was that the universe could be understood and controlled by our rational mind. Scientists used to say to themselves, "Once we discover the rules, we can use them to determine our future, to shape what people do, to harness nature for ourselves." This became the hope for organizations. "Understand how humans behave, figure out how to manage that behavior and optimize it. Then design organizations that are highly efficient and predictable. Create the perfect structure, define jobs clearly, with small jobs fitting under the larger jobs in the organization chart. Then, put rewards and consequences in place to keep things under control." This is what management scientists used to say to themselves.

The view as we go into the 21st century is that nature, along with everything in it, isn't as predictable in its behavior as we thought. The dream of perfect control (a kind of stability) is a pipe dream. We can't determine what will happen in the future. We *can* influence it—but not in a way that gives us 100% certainty that what we want will happen. In fact, sometimes our attempts to influence things have consequences we never intended. For example:

◈ Executives dramatically reduce staff. This has an immediate positive impact on bottom-line performance because costs are less. But, because critical skills are lost, future innovation suffers. And lower morale reduces what other staff members contribute.

◈ Staff members take a "that's not my job" view when customers call with problems. In the short run, job boundaries are protected. In the long run, dissatisfied customers go to competitors. Business declines and staffing and promotion opportunities shrink.

If we dig deeply enough, we'll see the underlying belief in these two examples is flawed. It is the belief that we can control change by just solving the problem at hand.

It's time to examine this and other beliefs related to change—because we live in very complex times where even the very notion of change is changing. That's the purpose of Part I. Use it to help you examine your beliefs and, if necessary, to modify them.

So what do you believe about change? As you read the sections that follow, reach *deep* into yourself to find the beliefs that *really* influence what you do. As you do this, know that there are two types of beliefs:

SAY beliefs: the beliefs you TALK about having

DO beliefs: the beliefs that actually DRIVE YOUR BEHAVIOR

As you think about your beliefs, notice that the beliefs you need today are not the "opposite" of yesterday's guiding principles. Most of the time, they include an old belief and put it into a new perspective.

Before you go on, I suggest that you take the "What Is Your Empowering Belief Quotient?" self-test at the end of Part I. It will help you surface your beliefs and relate your own thoughts to the chapters that follow.

SAY VS. DO BELIEFS...

What is 'Normal'

OLD BELIEF:		NEW BELIEF:
Stability is normal. *Change is an exception.*		*Both stability and change* *are normal.*

YOU ARE A BLEND of stability and change. Your genes, your history, your capabilities, all have an ongoing identity that is YOU. An organization is the same way. But you and the company you keep are also constantly changing. The trick is to change fast enough—in a way that keeps you growing and successful, without losing your own center and sanity.

Today, the pace of change is accelerating. This makes it more important to adapt to and influence change. Ironically, it also makes it more important to know and value what makes you, YOU; what makes your organization what it is today.

While change is a popular topic, so are stability topics like "vision," "purpose," and "core capabilities." The irony of accelerating change is that it requires us to see change and stability as two sides of the same coin.

This parallels an amazing scientific discovery of the 20th century: we used to think that energy and matter were different things. Now we know that energy and matter are two expressions of the same thing. A particle (matter) can also be a wave (energy). Think of what happens in nuclear bombs—as small amounts of matter are suddenly broken apart to create all that energy.

LIFE IS STABILITY AND CHANGE

The lesson? Each of us must be both a particle (something stable) and a wave (something changing), whether at work or at home and in the community. Neither change nor stability can exist without the other—for us personally, for us at work, or for organizations.

What are YOUR "DO" Beliefs about "What is Normal?"

If you frequently talk like this . . .

"I can't wait until this is over so we can get back to business as usual."

"Let's go back to what worked for us in the past."

Then, your beliefs may be holding you back.

Try to shift to a NEW way of thinking . . .

"Let's use this old system as an anchor while we make these changes."

"I want to stay up-to-date on the changes going on around us so I can prepare for them now."

"I'm doing my job well today, but what about tomorrow? I want to stay up-to-date so I can be as good tomorrow as I am today."

An old shop steward, who had been one of the most vocal resisters in an organization-wide empowerment initiative, stood in front of his peers and senior management. His words? "It's taken me some time to realize it, but I had—and have—a lot to learn. For the first time in many years, I feel excited to come to work. But I'm retiring in six months. I only hope that others will take some risks and get more involved after I'm gone."

On Resistance and Negative Emotions

OLD BELIEF:

*Resistance and negative emotions
sabotage change.*

NEW BELIEF:

Resistance is a wake-up call.

RESISTANCE AND EMOTIONAL RESPONSES to change are not bad. They are a signal to pay attention. They are a sign that forces are gathering to shift relationships and move NEW behaviors into the mainstream.

Think of resistance and negative emotions as "persistence energy." They are stability's voice crying out to test the value of a change.

Your resistance belief (Belief #2) relates to your "what is normal" belief (Belief #1). It reflects your view of the normalcy of change. When you believe that "stability is normal; change is the exception," then resistance and negative emotions carry a lot of power. They are a fearsome force: a battle call to protect your ego, to ward off all information and pressures for change, to protect you from annihilation.

However, when you believe that "stability dancing with change is normal," then resistance is only one voice in an important dialogue. It is neither good nor bad. It says: "Here is what it may be important to preserve." "Here are capabilities to continue to use." "Here are strengths I need to leverage." "Here are essential parts of my identity to look at and bring into the future." "Here's a sensitive personal area, so tread softly."

Your resistance and negative emotions may also be saying: "Develop something new—a new perspective, a new belief, some new capabilities." "Get rid of some things, clean out your life and your work closet." "Move away from some old behaviors and beliefs." "Now is the time to challenge thinking you took for granted as a child." "Replace old beliefs with something more vital for the future."

In other words, your resistance and anxiety may be saying, "Now is time for you to take a step into the unknown—to take some risks!!"

For people leading change, resistance from others (including yourself) is a SIGN that something important to people is going on. It is a reminder to respect the strengths and assets that come from the past. Resistance is a call to reframe old qualities and help them serve new purposes. It contains messages about how to design a change so that it can be successful.

"When we shift into more team-focused work, we will lose our high-performing individuals," the resistance voice says, coming from a "win-lose" belief system.

But there is a lot of good energy under this. The challenge is to create a team environment where performance is highly valued and where people are appreciated and challenged. High-performing individuals can help design it.

If you feel that you are a VICTIM OF CHANGE, resistance and negative emotions are signs to call your will into service—to become really *conscious*. Resistance is a response to feeling threatened. It usually starts as something subtle and unconscious—a feeling, a loss of energy, a disconnection. The natural reaction is to fight and defend, run away, or freeze and comply. You may even try doing more of what you did successfully in the past, faster, with more vigor. In other words, you'll act as though change is "abnormal." All of these reactions can hurt you in the long run.

On the other hand, if you believe that "resistance and negative feelings are useful signals," you'll see resistance and emotional reactions as wake-up calls. They are signs to appreciate what has worked in the past. But they are also signs to look with fresh eyes at what's around you. And they may be signals to open up to doing something new and getting rid of something in you that might be outmoded or dysfunctional.

RESISTANCE AND NEGATIVE EMOTIONS

Of course, resistance and negative emotions can be signs that you need to take a stand *against* a change. Some changes may be positive in the short term, but have net negative effects in the future. If you feel this is true, then you might decide to resist change.

There is no formula for when to decide to support or resist a change. The important thing is to explore new information and make your choice thoughtfully. Being this open and aware is pretty tough, but it's the best course of action! To do it, you need to explore resistance and negative emotions and understand them before you act.

What are your "DO" Beliefs about "Resistance and Negative Emotions?"

If you frequently do things like . . .

React without thinking when something changes around you.

Feel inadequate and stupid when something changes, and then think, "I shouldn't feel this way."

Look for ways to manage and control others' resistance to change.

Keep change and conversations about change on a rational, factual plane, avoiding emotion.

Run away from or fight change without taking time to see its future benefits.

Let your emotions and fears take over and run the show.

Then, your beliefs may be holding you back.

Here are some alternatives . . .

Acknowledge signs of resistance and negativity in yourself or others, without judging.

Ask, "What's really at risk here? What is the resistance (mine and/or others') trying to protect? What's the long-term benefit of protecting it? If there is none, how can I/we let go of what's being protected—with respect and dignity for the person or group feeling threatened?"

Ask, "What is this resistance telling us about things we have to do to make this a long-term success?"

Ask, "Is this change creating dilemmas—for me or others—that need to be addressed?"

Then you'll be positioned for success as things change in the new world of work.

A Senior Executive in a major corporation initially supported a new Performance Management process that would bring more information and participation to everyone. Her "say beliefs" supported initiatives like this. However, as the program began to roll out, it became clear that she had to become more aware of her use of her rank and power. She also had to take time to educate people about the business, to delegate, and to let go. She was used to being in charge and inventing ideas herself (her "do" beliefs). Her resistance was obvious to others, but not to herself. She tightened up control and found many things to criticize in her teams' and others' work. When she was challenged, she used rational arguments: "My people aren't ready." "They are very dependent." "They need close supervision." "Their ideas aren't what I would do."

Faced with her control, the people around her went back to "business as usual." People were once more dependent, and her beliefs became a self-fulfilling prophecy. She had lost an opportunity to "use" her resistance energy. It may have been telling her to help her staff develop self-management skills. Instead, she killed a process that could have helped both her and her staff to grow.

Years ago, I was privileged to work with a master of production technology in my company. He frequently complained about his equipment: "It isn't fast enough." "It's too hard to train people on this." But when we decided to purchase a new set of equipment, the production head suddenly became the biggest supporter of the old way. He began to tout the strengths of the old equipment—even kept track of its speed and accuracy compared to the new. Eventually, though, he adopted the new technology and became one of its staunchest supporters. But it took some time. "I was disoriented," he said. "I thought my job was gone. Now I see that my own fears blinded me to this really powerful breakthrough."

His resistance slowed his acceptance. But his *persistence* energy—his ability to be committed to a direction—became a strength. He became a strong supporter of the new method once its benefits were clear. AND his concerns helped us adapt the new technology to our special needs.

Executives in a major telecommunications company faced traumatic challenges from new and growing competitors as Internet markets heated up. This changing landscape clearly called for a new, more partnering relationship with the company's major unions. But most of the executives grew up under a "win-lose" union-management ethic. They'd been trained to win by either "sucking the union dry" or by treating it as a necessary evil. Management also let the union manage the frontline people in the business. Their adversaries on the union side had a similar "win-lose" history and supported the 'disconnect' between management and workers. In the meantime, as the entire industry changed, many small companies and some formidable competitors took market share. Global players swarmed into previously protected space. In the midst of a changing landscape, the management-union relationship prevented the company from adopting more modern and participative management methods. Shareholder trust dropped, other companies lured top talent away, and the company launched many painful downsizing programs. Both the company and the union suffered a loss of credibility that may never be restored.

What if either or both management and union had said, "This is a really new era—how can we both win? How can we work together to create a new communications future?" Resistance and fear destroyed an opportunity to move the industry in an entirely new direction. It made it possible for competitors to establish strong roots. And surely, the resistance to change is a key factor in making the company a poor investment bet early in the 21st century.

When Change Starts

Change starts when we plan it or are forced to change.

Change starts before we see it.

A major change happened in South Africa in 1994—the year of the first democratic elections, the year that brought Nelson Mandela's party into power. When you hear people outside of South Africa talk about the changes there, they cite 1994 as the beginning of that change. Some people in the United States would say it started with sanctions levied in the 1980s. Change always seems to start when we become conscious of it.

But the current changes in South Africa can be traced back to the mid-1900s and earlier—to courageous actions by people in prisons; to committed actions by some business leaders who saw apartheid as an economic disaster; to debates, dialogues, and personal leadership by church leaders, young and old people of all races in and outside the country; to pressures to participate in a global economy. Some of the change actions seemed like failures at the time. But they were all part of a run-up to the massive change that burst forth into the mainstream in 1994.

FUNDAMENTAL CHANGES START LONG before we are aware that a new direction will actually become the mainstream. These changes often start as "failed" projects (Post-it Notes started as a glue that didn't permanently stick), as actions by a minority (The makers of the first PC's couldn't sell them to Xerox). Or they start as shifts in normal patterns that we deny or don't even notice (Think about how fast the INTERNET crept up on us!). A reliable client base starts to erode. Processes that worked in the past begin to falter. People start to resist or criticize a management style that was always accepted in the past.

Closer to home, think about your own health. Problems start long before you recognize them. Many health problems exist as genetic tendencies—there before you were born. They may start as habits that will lead to trouble. Or they may start as dissatisfactions with lifestyle or work that fester in your subconscious and ultimately cause disease. You may go on a special diet, and fail. You may try to stop smoking, and fail. Then, illness strikes and you are forced to pay attention. The illness may be the first time you are even aware there is a problem. But, clearly, the illness is just a noticeable signal in a string of events that started long before.

Now that change is accelerating, we don't have the luxury of missing the subtle clues that change is happening or is needed. We don't have the luxury of denying the need for change just because past efforts "failed" to move into the mainstream. This doesn't mean that every change we hear about is worth supporting. But it does mean we need to be more aware and alert. Tomorrow's big changes already exist as little sparks and failures around us today.

So challenge your beliefs that change starts when you decide to start it, or when you are forced into it. And challenge your conclusions that failed initiatives of the past are not worth pursuing today. Those initiatives (often called "fads," "been there before's") may have been the first sprouts of a major new crop. They may have been trial balloons, unplanned alpha and beta tests, lucky mutations (mistakes), opportunities to practice and build new skills for the real race that lies ahead.

Start believing—knowing—that change starts subtly. Your task is to become more aware. Notice things earlier. Pay attention to shifts in the environment, changes in how things work, deviations from old

SUCCESS OFTEN BUILDS ON FAILURE

patterns. When new programs and ways of doing things appear, think, "why is this coming up right now?" rather than "another flavor of the month. . . . I'll wait and see if it is successful."

When you notice you are thinking, "We tried something like that before and it failed," ask instead, "Why is this coming up again?" "What's important about this that we need to do in order to develop and be successful in a changing environment?" "How is the situation different today from when we tried this before?" "Did we learn anything last time (when we 'failed') that can help us be successful now?"

The point is not whether something failed in the past. Failures are a necessary precursor to future success! The key consideration is: what needs to be done today and for the future? Broaden your awareness of change to include the subtle clues and early projects that created the path to today. If you believe that "important changes start subtly and with early failures," your attitude, reactions, ideas, and conversations about what's happening around you will take a dramatically new form.

What are your "DO" Beliefs about When Change Starts?

If you frequently do things like . . .

> Decide when a change is introduced, "We did that in the past and it didn't work." (This may be true, but perhaps the timing wasn't right and there wasn't enough energy for breakthrough to success.)

> Say about a change, "I (you) did it! . . . I (you) made this happen!" (This disregards all the past efforts and failures that probably led to the current success.)

> Walk away from a goal or a vision because something you tried to do failed. (Maybe the future will show that what you tried to do earlier was the first trial balloon of something very important!)

Try to shift to the NEW way of thinking . . .

> When things you or others try to do fail, reexamine if the purpose is worth pursuing and committing to. Then look for ways to keep the idea alive and to build on what you learned.

> Listen for new ideas and minority points of view that may be signs of an emerging change. Appreciate that something new may be arising—even if you don't agree with it. "Notice things" as they begin to happen.

> When someone says, "We tried that before, it didn't work," ask yourself, "Is what we now plan the 'right' thing to do?" If you think it is, identify ways that the past "failure" actually helped pave the way for this new thing to be a success. (The past "failure" may have

developed useful skills, identified problems to solve, created awareness if not action, etc.)

Then you will be positioned for success in a changing world of work.

A company had tried to introduce a sophisticated computer system to link many of the business functions. But training was inadequate, the system itself had a lot of glitches, and the culture (which favored silos rather than cross-unit cooperation) killed it. It was an expensive mistake. Two years later, a new president introduced "another" integration package. Fortunately, the beliefs of many associates about failed projects had shifted.

In the past, they would have said: "This will never work here. We tried that and it was a miserable failure. I'll wait and see with this one." Now the conversation goes: "The timing wasn't quite right for this back then. We now know what the lack of cross-unit cooperation is costing us—partly thanks to that failed experience (we're more aware of these issues because we tried and failed!). It will be easier to implement the new system because we developed some skills then that we can use now—and we won't have to start from scratch!"

In 1990, a member of a small network of professional colleagues tried to get the group to develop an on-line way of communicating using the Internet. The group looked into it and even tried some primitive programs. The project was cancelled—some members didn't have computers, some were afraid that the on-line communication would replace face-to-face meetings. And the technology was not reliable. People talked about the project as a "failure."

In 2000, this same group uses the Internet to keep the community together between meetings and to jointly plan meetings. It's only now clear that the experience in the 90s made it easier to adopt and use the technology today. The group was an early adopter of world-wide-web applications. The group's technology transformation actually started with that effort in the 90s, even though it didn't succeed at the time.

How Deliberate Change Happens

OLD BELIEF:		NEW BELIEF:

Change should happen in a sequential, planned, rational, and linear way.

Change moves in cycles and waves.

WHEN YOUR ORGANIZATION CREATES a strategy or a vision, it sets out on a path toward a deliberate goal. The often unspoken assumption (belief) is that this path of deliberate change will be the shortest distance to the goal, that it will be a straight line.

The same assumption applies to personal goals. Your expectation may be that, once you have a goal, all you have to do is behave in a way that achieves it. But this doesn't account for several facts:

♦ *Intentions and goals are only one cause* of behavior. Others are: the immediate situation, your current thoughts and attention, your energy levels, competing priorities, skill levels, what people and groups around you do and say, tools available, etc.

♦ The goal you want to pursue may be the *best you can articulate now.* But as you move toward the goal you may *discover* that you want to go somewhere else, create something else, do things differently. Experience and learning may tell you that what you want to do now will have some unacceptable negative long-term effects.

◈ The *urgency and energy for change may not be strong enough* to mobilize the change actions for breakthrough. So you may stay stuck—unable to leap to a new level and new way of working and being. It's like turning up the heat on a pot of water at sea level, but only to 200°F / 98°C: close, but not enough energy to boil!

◈ There are *different change forces at different times in a change process.* Early on, the old ways can make forward motion difficult. After all, the whole system is set up to support the current behaviors. It will resist like the body facing new bacteria—even if the bacteria will be helpful in the long run (e.g., help us better digest modern food). Also, *late* in a change process there are often massive resistance energies akin to the death throes of a

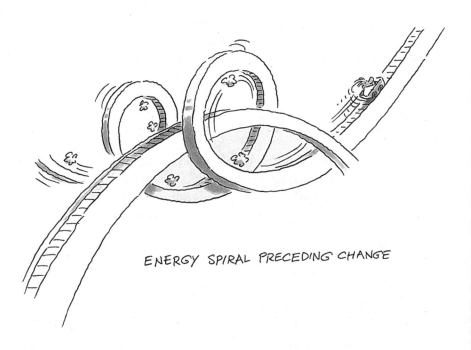

ENERGY SPIRAL PRECEDING CHANGE

mighty beast. This happens because "die hard" energies often mobilize for one last try to deflect change.

 For individuals learning new skills, there are *breakthrough periods and plateaus* (think about learning a new sport—the times of accelerated progress followed by prolonged periods of plateaus).

Rather than being a linear and progressive process, change goes through *cycles, eddies, and lurches*. As it moves, it often gathers the energy and wisdom to move from a marginal activity or idea into the mainstream.

Perhaps this is Nature's way of testing the viability and functionality of a change—of helping to hone and shape it so that it deserves to be in the mainstream. Like a mutation that becomes an ongoing feature in a species, a change has to prove it will add value for future survival.

What are your "DO" beliefs about how deliberate change happens?

If you frequently do things like . . .

Say, "This wasn't in our change plan. We must be on the wrong track."

Try to organize and control change efforts so that there is little left to chance.

Give up when the resistance and going get tough, saying, "this isn't going to work."

Give in and say, "Okay, whatever you want me to do, I'll do."

Consider shifting to a NEW way of thinking . . .

Notice when changes are happening without being formally or officially organized and controlled—and let them unfold to see what happens.

Try to keep the big picture and larger goals in mind, even when a change project gets stuck and seems to go backwards.

Try to sustain energy and optimism during flat periods and plateaus in a change that you or others are trying to make.

Make changes to the change plan when problems and learning say "do something more or different."

Explore whether strong resistances are a sign that major change is just around the corner—or a sign of something that needs to be re-thought about the change strategy.

Then, you will be positioned for success in a changing world of work.

When to Commit

OLD BELIEF:		NEW BELIEF:

Commitment follows success.   *Commitment drives success.*

"But the pay system isn't aligned."
"Our policies don't support this . . ."
"Our leaders aren't role models; when they are, I'll change."
"I'll commit when I'm sure this is going to happen."

THESE ARE ALL COMMENTS that come from an old belief system. Commitment to any change is most valuable and important when the outcome is NOT certain; when barriers and forces seem insurmountable. Commitment is the energy that makes dreams and visions come to life. It sustains action during the difficult and dark times. When you or anyone says, "I'll wait to commit," you take a stand for the status quo and cheapen the value of your commitment. "I'll wait to commit," says that you commit to things because others do—that you will go in the direction that the strong winds blow. Sailors know that this is a recipe for catastrophe!

Your view of commitment is a direct reflection of your stance about life and your power in it. Think about commitment in your personal life. Think about it in a marriage. It's easy to commit when things are going well—but not so easy when there are problems and the marriage's survival isn't assured!

At work, the old belief says that commitment happens when everything is set up for success, when everything is "aligned." In the old belief, commitment waits until they—the strategies, structure, policies, human resource practices, reward system, public personas, information and communication processes, leader behavior, budgets, and so on—are facing the same direction.

But think about it. These organization parts, like the various aspects of a marriage, are never in total alignment, as they would be in a mechanical device. Even in an organization that has grown gradually, developed a bureaucracy, and has a long-standing culture, the alignment will never be complete.

In a fluid organization—where there may be, for example, a big competitive or global threat—the alignment is always out of sorts. The strategies deliver one message; the operating practices support something else. Some pieces fit, others don't; some are old, some are new.

COMMITMENT IN UNCERTAINTY

Perfect alignment is, therefore, a myth—an aspiration. It is rarely, perhaps never, the truth.

Back to "commitment." These are the key commitment questions for you to answer when you realize that a major change is underway: "What is important here? "What does my organization need in order to be successful in the future?" "How is the environment changing?" "How must we change?" "What do I think is *RIGHT* for the future?" "Is this current change something that is important to support, or is it the 'flavor of the month' distraction?"

AND, the KEY questions: "What am I committed to as a player on this continually changing stage?" "How do I use my power and take care of myself in view of the misalignment of all the systems parts? (e.g., "The structure isn't right." "All leaders don't support this." "The pay system doesn't reward for this." "We don't have the tools and technology we need!")

As organizations of all kinds become more open and flexible, the opportunity for individual impact grows. Your commitment becomes more valuable than ever!

Nature in all its forms has a strong attraction to alignment, even though it can't ever fully achieve it in a living organism like a person, group, or an organization. Your commitment in uncertainty may be the force that brings things to a new level of capacity.

What are your "DO" beliefs about "Commitment?"

If you frequently . . .

Wait to support a change until you're sure it's going to happen.

Say things like, "When I'm convinced that leadership is behind this, I'll commit," or, "When the reward system supports this, I'll change," or, "Our policies say one thing and this new priority says something else. I can't change till this is sorted out."

Think, "My commitment doesn't matter anyway—I'm just one person."

Back away from changes you think are important when you see that leaders don't appear to be committed—or things like pay and promotion seem to reward something else.

Try to shift to a NEW way of thinking . . .

Imagine the kind of organization you would like to be part of—and that you would like to leave behind for others after you; support changes that will help create that kind of organization.

Take a stand for something because you think it's right, even when you are in the minority.

Have patience—or at least temporary tolerance—when everything doesn't fit or when parts of the organization don't align with a new direction.

Then you will make an impact in a changing world of work.

Many major social or organizational changes start with one or a few committed people. These people "buck" the system, take unpopular stands, or put out massive energy underground. They work long and hard without formal support and resources. This is such a key role in human nature that it is one of the major themes of religion, history, novels and movies: Moses, Jesus, Gandhi, Napoleon, Nelson Mandela, Lech Walesa, Mother Teresa, and Rosa Parks are among the really famous "change mavericks." Norma Rae, Oskar Schindler, and Erin Brockovich are immortalized in film for that role. All demonstrate the Chinese view that danger and opportunity are two sides of the same coin.

In the workplace, there are people who stand up for projects and changes they believe in, even if it seems dangerous to do so. They rally people behind them, put in their own energy when the organization won't provide resources, and get up again and again after setbacks. You know these people. Maybe you are one of them. They can surely say, "I stood for what I believed in," and perhaps even say, "My commitment made a big difference."

The Role of Formal Leaders

OLD BELIEF:

Formal leaders must drive change and be role models for the perfect and preplanned change process.

NEW BELIEF:

Leaders are co-learners in the processes of change.

A few years ago, in the midst of a large and complex change for one of the world's largest beer companies, I met with a group of union stewards to get their ideas about how to get associates more involved in the business processes. After quite a heated debate, one of the stewards said, "We are wasting our time. We can't change until THEY (senior management) change." After a hushed silence, I asked the group, "Do you think THEY can change?" Group response: "Yes, some of them." Question: "How many?" Group response, "About 50%." Question: "How long do you think it will take 50% to change?" Group response: "About three years."

At this point, I began to pack my things. From the group: "Where are you going?" My response, "I'll be back in three years." From the group: Silence . . . then, "But wait, if they show signs of changing, then we'll tolerate some mistakes."

The irony of this true story is that a few days later in a meeting with senior management, an executive said in frustration, "We can't change until THEY change."

ONE OF THE BIGGEST mistaken beliefs about major organization change—the kind of change that affects many people and requires new roles and relationships—is that one group must change before others. If the world and organizations were fully mechanical and rational, perhaps this would be possible. Someone or some group would *decide and plan a change and communicate it to others. They would* put the systems, structures, and rewards in place to get full alignment. *And then they would* educate and support everyone else to make changes in their behaviors. *Throughout all this, these "seers" would be* role models of courage, appropriate behavior, and rationality over resistance and emotions.

But expecting such perfection and control from leaders is unrealistic. The reality is that many of the demands of new markets, a global economy, and shifting technologies, are NEW to ALL of us. They require new leadership skills and behaviors AND new worker skills and behaviors.

Changes today require a new kind of learning and interaction amongst all players. Changes for one group dance with changes for others. Leaders can't play the change game alone. And THEY, too, must have space to learn.

Very few people in formal leadership roles were schooled in the INTERNET world. Few learned or saw role models of the leadership skills needed in what futurists Stan Davis and Chris Meyer call the BLURRED economy. And perhaps no one planned to lead a group of workers ranging from baby boomer pre-retirees, Gen X-ers, Hip-Hoppers, telecommuting workers, or a global workforce.

To expect perfect leader behavior under these conditions is to collude in creating an inhuman atmosphere—immobilizing the organization and its leaders. For "perfect" is an expectation that goes with the common belief (#1) that "stability is normal, change is the exception."

If you are a formal leader—someone with significant control over resources and strategies—you have some important ways to support change. For example, you can support and nurture possible new directions long before they move into the mainstream (some companies, like 3M, have leadership-supported ways to find and shelter new and even crazy ideas until they are strong enough to challenge the status quo).

And once there is a plan or goal for a change, leaders make a difference by bringing those changes into the mainstream, even though they don't have all the knowledge and skills to lead them once they occur.

It's also vital that leaders be active, aggressive LEARNERS. Their challenge is to rapidly and openly develop new leadership skills. Finally, it's vital that leaders USE their formal power wisely and consciously, for there will be times when they must make unpopular decisions and "pull rank" to serve the best interests of all stakeholders.

If you are an associate, a follower, an employee, a team member, then you have a right to expect formal leaders to be *committed* to the changes they espouse. You have a right to expect that formal leaders be *aggressive learners* so that they can play a strong and wise leadership role for the new world of work that's emerging. You have a right to expect that they will *take counsel* from people who can help accelerate their learning and challenge what they do. You have a right to expect that they will *listen to you and treat you as a partner in change*.

But be careful not to demand perfection. Remember, leaders are human and have irrational feelings just as you do. Don't lie in the wings looking for missteps. Avoid making your own learning and change dependent on what the formal leaders do.

Leaders are in a difficult position of trying to keep the organization together and performing during very challenging times. They've got to keep the business going while positioning it for a future that has only a fuzzy shape. And they have to juggle their own personal change challenges at the same time.

LEADER LEARNING AND REMAINING
COMMITTED TO THE GOAL

What are your "DO" Beliefs about the role
of formal leaders?

If you frequently do things like . . .

> Announce, *"The Director is not a role model of the change."*

> Say critically of people in power, *"What s/he does contradicts what s/he says."*

> *Feel insecure and blaming when you see your formal leaders do or say something that is at odds with a change that is going on.*

> *Look for imperfections and missteps in your leaders—contribute to gossip about their inadequacies.*

> Feel as a leader that *you have to be perfect, and therefore can't be a visible and active learner, taking counsel from others.*

> As a leader, *make verbal commitments to new directions but refuse to fund and resource them—expect the people in the organization to make change happen "on their own time."*

Try to shift to a NEW way of thinking . . .

> *Look across a variety of behaviors and comments by leaders to see if they are making real efforts to become better leaders—and/or support the deliberate changes going on in the organization.*

> *Tell formal leaders when you see that their behavior doesn't match their words or is inconsistent with a stated change goal. (e.g., "I am getting mixed messages from you about what is important. You said this . . . and did that . . . I'm confused, but must say that I am*

committed to the changes that are going on and I want to do the right thing."

Give leaders a period of time to have actions get more aligned with words and planned changes. If you see major resistance, raise the issue to someone you trust who can intervene.

As a leader, talk in public about what you are learning and how you are changing to meet shifting needs.

As a leader, counsel with people who have different perspectives, experience, and views—whether from inside or outside, up or down in the organization.

As a leader, act as a protector and supporter of major changes—even when short-term pressures demand a lot of your attention and resources; help release some of people's time and the organization's money for longer-term projects and culture/skill change efforts.

Then you are ready to make an impact on changes in the new world of work.

Several years ago, a large utility company launched a massive change effort—trying to bring more discipline and involvement into the organization. The Chairman was a key driver of the change. A big man, he was also quite feared by people in the business. There was always quite a bit of tension in management meetings. Months after the change process started, the Chairman was concerned about how people reacted to him and his rank. Since he admitted to friends that he was learning a lot, the advice to him was, "Let people in the organization know you are learning, too. This will help dispel the 'perfection myth' that surrounds you." He began to do this, and by taking this simple step, helped others see that they, too, could be learners. It unleashed a great deal of energy and experimentation—and quite a lot of surprise!

The Role of Followers

OLD BELIEF:		NEW BELIEF:
Followers have little power and can't be trusted to care about longer-term concerns.		*Followers have power.*

IN MANY PEOPLE'S CHANGE lexicon, change participants are divided into the "thinkers" and the "doers." The *thinkers* (leaders) plan the changes. The *doers* (followers) implement them—with minimum questioning and challenge.

By now it should be clear that roles are not as segmented as this implies. Yes, there is differentiation of function. Formal leaders do have the responsibility to create direction—to articulate and give resources to major change initiatives. But the "follower" is NOT a passive recipient and order taker.

In today's complex world, the members of any community both think and do for change. "Followers" (everyone is a follower in some way) play at least three important, active, and conscious roles.

First, there's the *INNOVATOR role*. As a community member, you give *early warnings and notice opportunities for change*. How is this true? People who are closest to the customer and operate in the value stream that creates, touches, and provides products and services, get clues about change all the time. These "edge" people often see new challenges and problems long before they are formal topics of strategy discussions in the Boardroom (remember Belief #3: When Change Starts!).

You can track many of the world's (and your own organization's) greatest innovations back to the learning that's happening on the front lines. But they have to be *noticed*. This is an important role for everyone—and for you—as you interact with customers, clients, and colleagues, and work with your organization's products and services. This is a call to a new level of consciousness—a new level of awareness and action. It's a call to notice new signals, and making them bigger and faster by talking to others about them and pushing for action.

A second role for you as a member of an organization, is to be a *SELF-MANAGER* of your own personal change dynamics. When change is going on, your current identity roles may be threatened. When this happens, you've got to notice and try to understand what is really going on for you. What will you have to give up if this change continues? What work will you have to do? What values and beliefs will you have to examine? Are there any stands you will have to take because your integrity demands it? How will you take care of yourself and participate?

And, a third role—once you feel that the change reflects a set of values that you can support—is to roll up your sleeves and be a *RISK-TAKER*. You now have a chance to move into a high gear of consciousness and learning. You have a chance to turn your automatic behavior switch to the "off" position. You may take risks by starting and leading a change. Risk-taking may also mean taking a stand for change while others around you are hesitant or resisting. That may mean taking a plunge into a new way of working where you personally might fail. Or being a risk-taker may involve taking a stand against any actions that—after serious reflection—you realize you can't support.

Learn, and watch your actions related to Beliefs #1 through 5 (about "what is normal," resistance and negative emotions," "when change starts," "how deliberate change happens," and "commitment"). Consider taking a stand *for* important change *before* you're thoroughly comfortable. Alternatively, be careful not to take arbitrary or defensive stands too soon. Stay open. Ask questions, listen, ask yourself "What if?" Explore what you are willing to give up in order to stay a member of the organization's community. Know where you must stand—at least for now.

Taking a stand requires a balance of being open and discerning—of listening and evaluating. Picture a switch on the wall. When it's in the up position, you listen—you see things from the other's view. When it's down, you evaluate. You can't listen and evaluate simultaneously. When it's time to listen and understand, flick the switch up by saying to yourself "I have to listen now." (Take a minute to imagine what it is like for you to really listen.) Then, after you've given yourself this space, flick the switch down and ask, "What do I think about this? How do I feel about it? What is defensive reaction and what is constructive?" Hard to do? You bet! But it's vital for emotional health and personal power.

FOLLOWERS
BEING PROACTIVE

Followership, "membership" is NOT a passive and receptive role where we have to do what others plan. But it does demand that we keep a perspective on both what is best for the organization (and, of course, all its stakeholders) and for us as members. It carries a responsibility to notice early signs of change, to process our own personal reactions and dynamics. And it requires all of us to be active, learning, and risk-taking participants in the change process itself.

What are your "DO" Beliefs about the role of followers?

If you frequently do things like . . .

> *Discount yourself as a powerless player in a larger game orchestrated by someone else.*
>
> *Take a reactive stance, either following orders OR refusing to participate in changes—without thinking.*
>
> *Leave the thinking and responsibility for the future to others—focusing just on your day-to-day work.*
>
> *Feel emotions about work like anger, blame, or resentment without trying to understand where they are coming from or what impact they are having on your behavior.*
>
> *Refuse to act on your ideas and things you are excited about because you are afraid to fail.*
>
> As a formal leader, *keep people in the dark and assume that you and other leaders must "take care of" workers or protect them from the truth or from change.*

Try to shift to a NEW way of thinking . . .

> *Think about what is going on around you so that you can influence ideas about options and the bigger picture.*
>
> *Appreciate your own feelings and reactions—even when they are negative. Then explore where they are coming from so you can either resist with integrity, or take some risks for your own growth.*
>
> As a formal leader, *treat the people who work in and around the organization as intelligent partners who can handle the truth, and*

who have ideas and important roles to play in shaping and implementing change.

Then you will continue to be a powerful shaping influence on the evolution of your organization—and you will use your work challenges to help you personally grow and develop, optimizing your life and contributions.

Henry Mintzberg, one of the world's thought leaders on organizations, challenges the traditional view of strategy. In the traditional view, people at the top or in specialist jobs study the environment and market, examine organization strengths and weaknesses, and propose strategies for the future.

Mintzberg says that this is ONE way to arrive at strategy. The OTHER is to capture innovations that are happening on the ground. He calls this "emergent" strategy. And guess how emergent strategy forms. It forms through the actions and reactions of the people who are doing the work. It forms because "followers" are trying new things, building on what works, and spreading the news.

The innovative, noticing, and risk-taking follower is actually a key strategist in any business. Everybody has power—to accelerate, to divert, to slow, and to reshape any change in any group they are part of.

Part I Conclusion

Our "do" beliefs create our world. They determine what we pay attention to. They affect how we act. They create consequences that are self-fulfilling prophecies. Notice the different outcomes below:

The *Vicious Cycle* outcome where beliefs create catastrophes:

> *I believe ("do" belief) that leaders must be perfect role models of the changes they talk about. I notice that they are not. I become cynical and refuse to commit to a change that—if I thought about it—is really a good one. Because I and others like me don't act and continue to criticize, leaders become defensive and less confident in their personal changes. The vicious cycle continues.*

The *Virtuous Cycle* outcome where beliefs create a new world:

> *I expect ("do" belief) the leaders to actively support the changes they are sponsoring, and to be trying to change themselves. I notice the things they do that are supportive and tell them that I appreciate them. If I need something else from them, I tell them that, too. I notice that my supportive actions are well received. My own commitment and willingness to risk grows. Noticing my changes, the leaders feel more confident that the organization can follow through. They increase their own efforts. A virtuous cycle occurs that accelerates the change process.*

Obviously, our own beliefs and behaviors don't *control* anything outside of us. But they are very powerful forces in the change mix.

Notice yourself—become as conscious as you can of your actions and the beliefs that drive them. Imagine what could happen if you practiced the NEW beliefs more often. If they don't change the organization, you'll at least create a better world for yourself and those around you to live in. Try it!

The following summarizes the concepts in Part 1 with a list of the "DO" Beliefs about change that we've covered.

7 Empowering Beliefs About Change

◈ BOTH stability and change are normal

◈ Resistance is a wake up call

◈ Change starts before we see it

◈ Change moves in cycles and waves

◈ Commitment drives success

◈ Leaders are co-learners

◈ Followers have power

What is Your Empowering Belief Quotient?

The following are common ways that people respond to change. Give each statement a rating to indicate how you ACTUALLY behave and think in situations where things are changing. Be honest. Focus on what you ACTUALLY say and do, not what you think you SHOULD say and do. This questionnaire is about DO BELIEFS! (And it's for your eyes only!)

> 5=I almost always think/do this
> 4=I frequently think/do this
> 3=I sometimes think/do this
> 2=I rarely think/do this
> 1=I never/almost never think/do this

_____ 1. I say/think, *"I want a job that's stable and predictable."*

_____ 2. I say/think, *"I can't wait until this is over so we can get back to business as usual."*

_____ 3. I say/think, *"I want to stay up-to-date on the changes going on around me."*

_____ 4. I say/think, *"I'll set up routines for what I can but still try to continuously improve."*

_____ 5. I notice my own resistance and negativity and try to understand it.

_____ 6. I try to keep change and conversations about change on a rational factual plane.

_____ 7. I tend to react without thinking when something changes around me.

_____ 8. I ask, *"What is this resistance telling me about things we have to do to make this a long-term success?"*

_____ 9. When things I or others try to do fail, I look for ways to learn and build on what I've learned.

_____ 10. I *say* when a change is introduced, *"We did that in the past and it didn't work."*

_____ 11. I *walk away from a goal or a vision when something I try to do fails.*

_____ 12. I notice and support trends before they are obvious to others.

_____ 13. I say, *"This wasn't in our change plan. Let's get back on track."*

_____ 14. I notice when innovations we didn't plan are happening and I give them room to grow and unfold.

_____ 15. I expect things to get gradually better and better when we are involved in a planned change project.

_____ 16. I try to keep the big picture and larger goals in mind, even when a project gets stuck and seems to go backwards

_____ 17. I *say things like, "When I'm convinced that leadership is behind this, I'll change."*

_____ 18. I think about the kind of organization I would like to be part of and support changes that will help create that kind of organization.

_____ 19. I say to myself, *"My commitment doesn't matter anyway. . . . I'm just one person."*

_____ 20. I take a stand for something because I think it's right, even when I'm in the minority.

_____ 21. I say critically of people in power, *"What s/he does con-tradicts what s/he says."*

_____ 22. I feel insecure and blaming when I see formal leaders do or say something that is at odds with a change that is going on.

_____ 23. I accept many failures in leaders as long as it is clear that they are committed to change and learning.

_____ 24. I compliment constructive changes I see in leader behavior or tell leaders when I am getting mixed messages about change.

_____ 25. (Rate only if you are a formal leader) I feel as a leader that I can be a visible learner when things change. I don't have to appear perfect, and therefore can be an active learner or take counsel from others.

_____ 26. (Rate only if you are a formal leader) As a leader, I make verbal commitments to new directions, but often don't properly fund and resource them. I expect the people in the organization to make change happen "on their own time."

_____ 27. I leave the thinking and responsibility for the future to others—focusing just on my day-to-day work.

_____ 28. I think about what is going on around me so that I can influence ideas about options and the bigger picture.

_____ 29. I often don't act on my ideas and things I am excited about because I am afraid to fail.

_____ 30. I manage myself to high standards of contribution— with little or no supervision.

_____ 31. (Answer if you are a formal leader) As a formal leader, I assume that I and other leaders must "take care of" workers or protect them from the truth or from change.

_____ 32. (Answer if you are a formal leader). As a formal leader, I treat the people who work in and around the organization as intelligent partners who can handle the truth about change and can help shape it.

Guide to Interpreting "What is Your Empowering Belief Quotient?"

It took some thought to respond to this questionnaire. Let's see what it may say that can guide you for more success in the future:

Do three things:

1. Develop an "old belief" "new belief" profile.
2. Find your "ally beliefs and practices"—the beliefs and practices that are part of the "new belief" system, and the beliefs and practices that may be hurting your ability to adapt and grow.
3. Decide what all this means for your future.

1. Develop an "old belief" and "new belief" profile

First, record your scores for each statement in the spaces below. And create a sub-total for each belief area:

1. _____
2. _____

3. _____
4. _____

TOTAL _____

Stability is the norm

TOTAL _____

Change AND stability are normal

5. _____

6. _____
7. _____

8. _____

TOTAL _____

Resistance sabotages change

TOTAL _____

Resistance is a wake-up call

9. _____

10. _____
11. _____

12. _____

TOTAL _____

Change starts with plans or crises

TOTAL _____

Change starts before we see it

13. _____

                  14. _____

15. _____

                  16. _____

TOTAL _____   _____

Change progresses linearly   Change moves in waves and cycles

17. _____

                  18. _____

19. _____

                  20. _____

TOTAL _____   _____

Commitment depends on success   Commitment drives success

21. _____
22. _____

                  23. _____

24. _____

                  25. _____ (leaders only)

26. _____ (leaders only)

TOTAL _____   _____

Leaders are role models   Leaders are co-learners
of the end state change

27. _____

                  28. _____

29. _____

                  30. _____

31. _____ (leaders only)

                  32. _____ (leaders only)

TOTAL _____   _____

Followers have little power   Followers make a key
                         difference in change

GRAND TOTAL _____   _____

       Old Beliefs   New Beliefs

Think for a few minutes about what your self-assessment says:

> If **"old" beliefs got more points than "new" beliefs,** then you are probably having a hard time with all the changes that are going on in today's world and workplace. You may be feeling a lot of stress; feeling out of control; yearning for the past. You may be helping prevent important changes—because your attitudes and beliefs may be infectious, spreading to others.
>
> Remember, though, that resisting change is **sometimes** appropriate. Sometimes taking a stand against change is a constructive thing to do. Sometimes stability is something to defend. But if you read the statements related to the "old belief" column, you will see that thoughtful resistance is a "new" belief strategy.
>
> If **"new" beliefs got more points,** then you are probably feeling like a participant in the massive changes occurring around and in us. If you have a high score in "new" beliefs, then you probably have a great inner strength that you can draw on—a self-confidence that helps you feel that you will thrive whatever the situation. This doesn't mean that you don't have emotions and fears—you probably feel them, and recognize and tolerate them more than people who have a higher "old" belief score. It does mean that you probably have the emotional and mental skills and stamina to swim in the turbulent seas of our world today and even enjoy the ride.

Think for a few minutes about what your overall score says to you.

2. Find your "ally" beliefs and practices. Discover both the beliefs and practices that support your success in the new world of work, and the beliefs and practices that may be hurting your ability to adapt and grow.

Here's a chance to get more specific.

First, find the beliefs below where you got the two highest "new belief" scores, and the two highest "old belief" scores. Place "x's" to indicate these.

#1: What is normal

    _____   *Old:* Stability is the norm. Change is an exception.

    _____   *New:* BOTH stability and change are normal.

#2: Resistance and negative emotions
_____ *Old:*   Resistance sabotages change.
_____ *New:*   Resistance is a wake-up call.

#3: When change starts
_____ *Old:*   Change starts when we plan it or are forced to change.
_____ *New:*   Change starts before we see it.

#4: How deliberate change happens
_____ *Old:*   Change should happen in a sequential, planned, rational, and linear way.
_____ *New:*   Change moves in cycles and waves.

#5: Commitment
_____ *Old:*   Commitment depends on success.
_____ *New:*   Commitment drives success.

#6: The role of formal leaders
_____ *Old:*   Leaders must be role models and drive the perfect and preplanned change process.
_____ *New:*   Leaders are co-learners.

#7: The role of followers
_____ *Old:*   Followers have little power and can't be trusted to care about longer term concerns.
_____ *New:*   Followers are Powerful in Change.

Now, look at the ratings you gave each individual statement in the Beliefs Questionnaire itself. Find the five statements you gave the most points to, and the five you rated the lowest. Write them here:

Top five rated items of "Old Beliefs"

Top five rated items of "New Beliefs"

Review all of the above and write a paragraph about YOU AND CHANGE that summarizes your insights. (E.g., "I am most likely to operate out of these beliefs and do these kinds of things" OR "This affects my flexibility and resilience (my life) in the following ways:")

3. Decide what this all means for your future.

There is no substitute for personal reflection here. You might want to take some time to answer the following questions:

◈ What changes will be happening around me in the next few years? How am I likely to respond? How would I like to respond?

◈ What is my life really about? What gets in the way of my expressing and living this purpose? What would happen if I lived as though I was a more powerful player in what is happening around me?

◈ What beliefs do I hold that are holding me back? What are the consequences of keeping these beliefs?

◈ What beliefs do I hold that are helping me be a player in the 21st century world? How can I draw on them more often?

◈ What one or two actions do I want to take as a result of this thinking?

PART II

Powerful Character

CHANGE IS A PART of life. So why do we seem more concerned about it now, in the early years of the new millennium?

Part of the reason is that we are becoming more powerful as a species. We have unleashed nuclear power, are unraveling the genetic code, and are manufacturing chemicals that warm the globe. At the same time, information technology, travel, and media touch even the poorest of us. Actions in one part of the world affect people in other places. The knowledge explosion takes us all into areas we never even knew existed. It opens doors to products, services, and ideas we could never have imagined even a decade ago. It shakes up our traditional retreats of family, church, and the old stability of our "job."

Increased power carries responsibility with it. Things like "change," that we took for granted in the past, are now something we have to think about—to make choices about. For change touches all of us—and we all influence it, whether we are aware of our role or not.

But what does this all mean to our lives? How do we, how do YOU *thrive in change?*

Part of the answer relates to who you ARE.

Character is something we develop all our lives. While it's not quite as easy to develop as skills, character is a matter of choice—and therefore something we can control.

Four CHARACTER actions are allies in change:

Take a stand
Know your beliefs and assumptions
Use your emotions
Add value in your world

Think, as you read, about who you ARE in these times where change helps define all of us. For whether at work, at home, or in your community, your character means as much or more today than ever before. Remember, these are times when one individual can infect the world's computers, determine presidential elections, trigger nuclear holocaust, infect thousands all over the world with killing disease, or launch causes that save millions.

As population, information, and technology increase and network, individuals (ironically) have more power than ever before. How able is our character—your character—to manage that power?

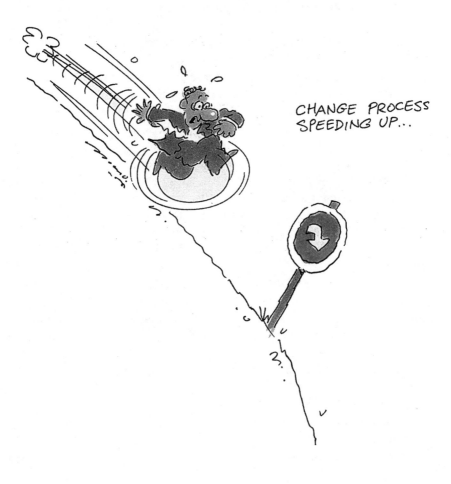

CHANGE PROCESS
SPEEDING UP...

Stand for Something

HAVE YOU EVER THOUGHT about the vast variety of interests and personalities there are in the world? The point came home to me years ago when my sons and I attended a "games" conference in Wisconsin. It was before the explosion of electronic games, but there were plenty of other options—from board games, to military games, to fantasy games. One session we chose was a version of a fantasy game where participants had to choose to be a character. The characters included wizards, warriors, thieves, kings, queens, trolls, and artisans.

I thought, "Why don't they just assign characters at random? After all, everyone will want to be a wizard!"

You guessed it! I was the only one who wanted to be a wizard. Others preferred different characters. I asked one boy why he chose to be a "thief." He said, "I want to be invisible in the night."

Now what does this have to do with change? Simply that we all have different preferences, views, and energies to bring to life. Some religious leaders, philosophers, and psychologists say that we come into the world with a purpose. Whether it's there from the beginning, or we develop our life purpose over time, or it evolves and changes through life, our sense of purpose is what creates meaning in our lives.

In addition, we all have different mixtures of abilities, preferences, and even values. The trick is to track down the driving force behind these abilities, preferences, and values—to find where your overall passion in life is. Mine is "to bring new life to organizations and to the people I love." When I am doing things that fit with this purpose, I am energized, courageous, at peace, and fulfilled. When I get off purpose, I am often tired and have to drag myself forward.

What do you stand for? What are your years alive all about? What will cause you to look back on your life and say, "I stood for something, and I feel good about it."

It's never too late to find and develop this part of your character.

TAKE A STAND...

A few years ago, during a management workshop in South America, the management team developed a new vision for their company. Several of the older executives dropped out of the discussion when we started to talk about changes in the leadership role. I went up to one of these people later and asked him what he was thinking. He said, "This has little relevance to me. I'm retiring in a year." I said, "What a great time to really take action, though. Think about it; you are in a position to set a new course for the company—to leave a legacy that will continue for years after you leave. Maybe you won't be here to see it, but if you don't act in the next year, you'll lose that chance for long-term impact."

This executive was in a position to make decisions, redirect resources, and take actions that would be felt by thousands of people for years. The span of his impact was longer than his time left with the company, but he could have let his retirement date interfere with his legacy.

The story has a happy ending. He spent his last year energetically developing several new leaders and helping prepare the business for a new direction.

Taking a stand sometimes requires us to separate our own immediate interests from our impact. But we have to know what we are about. In fact, in an age of accelerating change, it's really *important* to know what we are about. Otherwise, we are like feathers blowing in the wind. Remember *New Belief #1: Business As Usual is BOTH Stability and Change!* The stands you take are part of your stability—they anchor you so you can make a difference.

◈ When have you taken a stand? Have you ever taken a stand that you felt was personally risky? (E.g., could have cost you your job or something else very important to you?)

◈ What—in a sentence—is your life about? What is the essence of the meaning and legacy that is "YOU"?

◈ What are your highest priority values (e.g., family, impact, achievement, wealth, learning, recognition, service, affiliation)? What happens when, inevitably, your top values come into conflict with each other (when, for example, achievement and your family are in conflict)?

◈ Whom do you admire for having taken a stand? Why? What does this tell you about what is important to you?

Be Aware of Your Beliefs and Assumptions

CHRIS ARGYRIS, ONE OF the founders in the field of Organization Development (the study of how organizations change and adapt) wondered why, when we communicate with each other, we often don't tell the truth. He was curious about why we often say and do things that aren't the best way to react in a situation. He noticed that our "SAY" beliefs often were different from our "DO" beliefs!

"So," you say, "that there is a difference between 'say' and 'do' is not new news. Besides, we dealt with all this in Part I. Tell me something I don't know!"

But a minute, please . . .

There are lots of things going on when we communicate and when we act. Here are some of many things that can distort communication:

◈ Wanting to look good and trying to avoid guilt and shame

◈ Wanting to avoid hurting others—helping them avoid guilt and shame

◈ Not trusting the other person or the situation and communicating in a way that is safe for us

◈ Responding to some indirect message from the other person (to a tone of voice, body language, a choice of words)

◈ Projecting feelings from our own past (the other person may remind us of a mean relative—and so we react as though to the relative)

◈ Reacting from an unconscious belief system (e.g., coming from an authoritarian belief system, we may withhold information from or abuse someone we lead—or we may wait to be told what to do)

◈ Not being aware of our own real feelings, needs, and intent

All of these track back to assumptions, to "beliefs." The problem is, these assumptions are often unconscious. You may be aware of what you are saying—and perhaps how you are feeling—but totally unaware of the assumptions behind your words and feelings.

Some years ago, the psychologists Azjun and Fishbein—experts in how beliefs and values form and influence behavior—wrote an interesting book called *Beliefs, Attitudes, Intentions, and Behaviors.*

They showed how:

A **belief** (*e.g., "change is abnormal"*) turns into **several attitudes** (*e.g., negative attitude toward and fear of change, negative attitude toward people who want change*). These attitudes, in turn . . .

> lead to **many intentions** (*"I'll resist any change that will affect my job," "I'll ignore changes; see them as fads," "I'll expect proof that the changes will happen before I commit."*) And then, these intentions ultimately . . .

> > turn into **lots of actions** (sabotage, illness, refusal to learn, blaming, etc.).

The key is to be aware of the assumption or belief that is behind the attitudes, intentions, and actions.

I BELIEF

SEVERAL
ATTITUDES AND
INTENTIONS

MANY BEHAVIORS

BELIEFS → ATTITUDES → INTENSIONS → BEHAVIORS

"But how," you might ask, "can I know a belief if I'm not conscious of it?" And, "Why is it important anyway?"

Last question first: it's important to try to know our fundamental assumptions and beliefs because they influence a lot of our thinking, feelings, and actions. In a big way, they create our view of our life, relationships, and work!

And these beliefs may either be out of date or just not good for us today. For example, it is just not useful to carry *authoritarian* or dependent beliefs anymore. In this age of instant information and participation, controlling bosses and dependent workers can't keep up with new insights and demands. So they are headed for failure!

Now to the first question: "Can I know a belief if I'm not conscious of it?" The answer is yes, but you have to be a bit of a detective. Here are some clues to look for. Notice:

◈ Situations where you often feel uncomfortable and less effective

◈ Problems that come up over and over again

◈ Extreme negative or extreme positive reactions to certain ideas, individuals or groups of people

◈ Times when you act in a defensive way

When these things happen, ask yourself, "What did I do or say?" "What were my intentions?" "What attitudes were behind the intentions?" "What beliefs and assumptions might be behind what I did or said?" "Are these beliefs valid, or do I need to change or replace them?" (In the spirit of what you learned in Part I about "*say*" beliefs and "*do*" beliefs, be careful to focus on what actually drives behavior—on what you *do,* not what you *preach!*)

One way to do this is to ask a series of "why" questions.

"I was just rude to several people in the meeting." (An <u>action</u>)

Why? What were my <u>intentions</u>?

"To look good and make my point of view seem more valid."

Why? What <u>attitudes</u> were behind this?

"I react positively to arguments that have lots of statistics and seem rational. I distrust emotional and non-scientific information. The people I was rude to used emotional and subjective arguments."

Why do I feel this way about rational and emotional arguments? What <u>beliefs</u> are behind this?

"Organizations and people—at their best—are rational and scientific. I must always be a model of what is 'best.'"

It is a matter of character to try to understand what is driving our behavior. All of us interact with (and therefore, influence) many people every day. We are responsible for the effects of our interactions. And we do have the ability to notice and understand what drives us.

The next great frontier is the frontier of the human mind and emotions. In order to thrive in change, can we—even now—gently and creatively begin the journey into our own!!

◈ Think about decisions you made in the last month. What do they say about your assumptions/beliefs?

◈ What problems keep coming up for you—over and over again? What do you do/think/feel/say when they happen? Now, ask yourself WHY you act and react the way you do. Ask "why" until you finally come to a belief.

"Why do I get defensive and angry when others challenge my views?"
"Because I don't want to feel inadequate!"
"Why don't I want to feel inadequate?"
"Because I want to be seen as a competent person!"
"Why do I want to be seen as a competent person?"
"Because being competent is essential to being accepted!!"
"Why do I want to be accepted?"
"Because other people's views are what determine my value!!"

BINGO!!!! THIS IS THE BELIEF!!!!!

"What if I changed my belief about what makes me valuable to, for example, 'I am the judge of my own value'?"

Use Your Emotions

TIMES ARE CHANGING. We now realize that *emotions* are a big part of being human. Furthermore, we NEED to bring our emotions to work. They are the energizers of creativity, commitment, risk-taking, innovation, and great leadership. Rather than apologize for and hide emotions, we've got to learn how to unleash their energies while keeping them from abusing others.

Anxieties, excitement, fear, passions, resistance, defiance, conflict, commitment—all are emotions—"sources of motion!"

Strangely enough, we have learned to suppress these powerful forces. We've learned that they are out of place in the workplace! We talk about "controlling conflict," at the same time as we yearn for breakthrough thinking and energy. When changes occur, our emotions come out in force, but so do our controls and taboos.

"Tame and suppress feelings!" says our politically correct organization self.

But think about it! When we *feel* anxiety—when we *feel* resistance and concern—we are actually being called to life.

Consider facing these situations: reorganization, strategy or market changes, new technologies or processes, being asked to join several new teams. A change happens or threatens to happen in your personal life. You feel queasy. You feel called to defend the status quo. You want to protect what you know "works." The feeling seems to scream, "Stop this change!"

But, what if the *feeling* is actually a call to consciousness? What if it is saying, "Pay attention . . . Something important is happening." "A learning experience is about to occur." "Something is changing . . ." What if the feeling is saying "It may be time to test a belief"—for your belief (that this is dangerous) may be what is evoking the feeling.

In these early moments of facing change, it's not clear what to do or how to react. Should you resist and shut down—batten the hatches and get out the cannons to defend the status quo? Or should you hold out your shield for a bit of protection and move forward, carrying a white flag to the center of the field, not to surrender, but ready to listen to a new proposition?

Another complication is that a change may be happening—but it might be in its very early stages. If you are a very courageous sort, you will jump into the front lines and become a champion—against what may be heavy odds. If you are a bit more conservative, you will wait, get yourself ready for a new era, and join forces with others when they march right past your house. You then join the movement once it has mass and momentum.

But if you are very timid and not sure about what you stand for, you may hide or resist. Or, if you clearly stand for the status quo, you may launch a counter-operation.

EMOTIONS ARE A SIGNAL

There is no obvious "right" answer. Some people did stand and fight against Hitler's "new order." (They stood for a kind of old "status quo.") Others did take courageous stands against South Africa's apartheid regime (They fought the "status quo.") I've seen courageous people take a stand against a new technology because the changes would make the organization less customer-friendly. Often these stands lead to different decisions and actions.

It's not always clear what to do with anxieties and emotions, or when to act on them. But it's important to recognize when we feel uncomfortable, resistant, defensive, and to see that these are signs that something important is happening.

Emotions are always a wake-up call to take a stand one way or another; a wake-up call to challenge assumptions and to learn. Our emotions are a wake-up call to say, "Wait, consider this before you move!" "Be careful here!" Always, they are a wake-up call to think and move to another stage of aliveness.

Emotions are sometimes a signal to challenge our comfort zones, to reach to the depths of who we really are, to tap into the energy reserves we keep for our defining moments.

They are also part of what unites us with the people around us. They are a call to community. They say that you don't have to handle this alone—because what you are feeling is probably what others are going through, too!

So your emotions may feel like resistance at first—and resistance may be the best initial and/or final reaction. But until you examine your emotions and look at what is triggering your discomfort, be careful not to misinterpret the message. You certainly don't want to think that a positive change is a threat! Since emotions don't initially distinguish between positive and negative change, this is a danger. Be sure to take time to think before you act. Remember that life is both change and stability—and that some of life's greatest threats are its most glorious opportunities.

One organization decided to change its performance management system from one that focused on appraisals by managers to one that used feedback from customers and key receivers of individuals' work. The new process also made individuals responsible for managing their own feedback process. Afraid of a loss of control, many managers resisted the new process. In discussions with them, we tried to get to the source of the resistance. Beliefs about people ("they are not trustworthy"), and confusion about the manager's role surfaced as important issues. Together, we clarified the manager's role and authority and identified many situations where employees had taken responsibility on their own. We looked at the common problems of traditional performance appraisal systems (game playing, withholding information, managers' discomfort with making judgments) and we compared them with what might happen under the new system. And we designed some support to help managers and workers develop important skills for success.

For many people, resistance led to plans for a more successful implementation.

Anyone who has lived through a terrible trauma and found very positive change on the other side knows what this lesson is all about. But the challenge is to take that learning into future situations.

The point is that emotions are a signal that something important is happening. It's seldom initially clear whether they are a warning or a welcoming signal. As a person of "character," you just need to see strong feelings as a SIGNAL—to notice and eventually act.

◈ When you feel threatened and uncomfortable, how do you react?

◈ What do you want to do with sudden surges of defensiveness, anxiety, and threat? How can you take care of yourself and still see the real message in the "threat"?

◈ Can you think of a time when you felt very defensive and threatened, met the challenge, and came out in a much better place? What happened to allow that to occur? How did you get through the difficult times?

◈ What is happening right now in your personal or work world that may change your life in some way? Are you reacting to it as a threat or as an opportunity? What can you do to give yourself some breathing room to explore it with more perspective?

◈ Take the biggest threat that you face today. If you had to, how would you turn it into a growth experience—an opportunity?

◈ If a challenge you feel anxious about is clearly a "bad thing"— how can you turn your anxiety/concerns into first, an insight, and then if necessary, a stopping force?

Add Value in Your World

THINK ABOUT THE PEOPLE you want to be around: the people who influence your life. Think about the people you want to follow, be friends with, or be like. What are they like?

Most of us are attracted to people who have hope, optimism, and a can-do view of life. We like energy—we all want to be ALIVE.

If change is something that we simultaneously participate in and co-create—then energy is involved.

The old view was that the universe was a big mechanical system governed by big rules, competition, and "natural selection" where we had little influence and where the future was pretty much predetermined. The best we as humans could do was to try to understand the rules, enforce them, and ride along.

Now, scientists believe that, although the universe (and the organization) is becoming more complex all the time, there are lots of possible ways to evolve. What decides the direction? Lots of things, including our own actions. We CO-CREATE, but we may never truly know the magnitude of our impact. (Did the inventor of Post-Its know his impact when he noticed that a new glue wasn't bonding permanently?)

Scientists today talk about the "butterfly effect:" the ultimate *optimistic* statement! They say that a single butterfly flapping its wings off the coast of Africa can set in motion a hurricane off the coast of Florida.

But the wing-flapping may just dissipate into thin air.

The challenge to each of us is to "flap our wings" with spirit and gusto. We make a huge difference in small and sometimes very large arenas. Like the grain of sand that finally topples a sandpile, we may experience the impact of our ideas and actions. But the second to the last grain of sand on the pile was important, too. Optimism and hope build on each other!

ADD VALUE... MAKE A DIFFERENCE

The Practicalities

The point in this character lesson is: act, work, and live your life as though you do make a difference.

How does this happen? Where can our little actions actually have impact? Think about the impact of these behaviors:

Appreciation. Positive feedback (appreciation) has an enormous "multiplier" effect. You are much more likely to make something happen if you appreciate what's working than if you punish what is not working. (Why? Because punishment has many negative emotional consequences. It causes people to withdraw and get defensive!)

Many important and dramatic changes in life occur because something *NEW* is *supported and appreciated.* Think about it: A leg sprouts on that first land-hugging fish. It helps the fish straddle the dry world—and therefore gets what we call *positive reinforcement.* The natural tendency of the fish body is to say—"WRONG. Fish don't have legs." But rather than *negative reinforcement* ("WRONG"), the new leg gets a "Hooray . . . . what fun . . . . a new capacity . . . . I CAN WALK!!" The leg provides what we now call "evolutionary advantage!" Evolutionary change sometimes goes unnoticed and unappreciated for a very long time.

If you have children, then you know that your positive and appreciative actions carry a great deal of power that actually unleashes energy and self-confidence. Negative feedback and controls—these are necessary sometimes—can destroy children if there is not an overall environment of appreciation. Far too many of us learn this lesson the hard way!

Hope and Optimism. These are forces that stimulate, magnetize, and magnify change. They capture and evoke the human spirit. Virtually every Olympic athlete, every great leader, and many survivors of terrible accidents and terminal illnesses are HOPEFUL and OPTIMISTIC. They think about their goal. They think about winning. They focus on the purpose in their lives. They imagine going beyond the obstacles. They sometimes even make the barriers and threats their "friend." They laugh, think hopefully and optimistically. Whether they win or lose (and they often win), their lives are better for being hopeful. And the people who are their allies have huge impacts on the course of their success.

It doesn't take a genius to realize that positive feedback and optimism, hope and respect, are key to rapid change in ourselves, others, businesses, and communities everywhere. Yet many of us are afraid to be a beacon of light and optimism. Why not stand out there and say, "Hey, this is the right thing to do!" "That took courage." "We can do this, even though it looks impossible." "You did a great job." "You gave it a try, even though it didn't work." "So this one didn't work. What did you learn that you can use in the future?" "This is the right thing to do, even though it's hard." "This takes courage, but you can do it!"

IMPACT OF POSITIVE & NEGATIVE EMOTIONS

The world of business and organizations—and human societies in general—go overboard on negative feedback. This triggers emotional defensiveness and fear that then inhibits future success.

Why not be a voice of optimism and hope? Of positive feedback? You don't have to be a Pollyanna—only saying nice things. You don't have to be insincere and manufacture compliments that aren't based on fact. But the world and businesses are full of so much negative and corrective feedback that we really don't have to worry too much about getting the "positive" out of balance. Think of the T-shirt: "Success comes in cans, not can'ts."

You'll find your role in change will dramatically shift when you bring more light than punishment, more ideas than criticism. Consider bringing "can do," and "did" in greater proportions to "can't do," and "failed." The issue is proportions (say, three or four optimistic to every one pessimistic comment and action). It's never "either-or."

❖ How do the people who work with you see you? As a negative force who always opposes change, or as mostly optimistic, hopeful, and open about the the future?

❖ How do you try to influence others? Through criticism, judgments, lecturing? Or do you talk about how their behavior affects you and seems to affect others?

❖ What do you think is your ratio of positive to negative or judging comments to colleagues; that is, what % positive and supportive, and what % negative and critical?

❖ For one week notice your comments and their impact on others—negative and positive. Notice how people react and what happens (in your relationship and in their behavior) as a result.

❖ How do you see yourself? As an optimist? A pessimist? There are benefits to both—but what do you gain and lose by being more one than the other?

❖ How does your tendency to make positive vs. negative statements affect your participation in the things that are changing around you? How does it affect your role as a leader for the future?

As you leave the Character lessons, think about who you want to BE in change. How can you be a person who *takes a stand?* A person who is *aware of your beliefs* and assumptions? A person who uses your *emotions as a call to consciousness?* Someone who *cares to add value* to the world and people around you? Imagine yourself being more and more this kind of person.

Then, for contrast, imagine what it would be like to be the *opposite*—someone who retreats from change. Someone who lets unconscious beliefs, perhaps from childhood, rule the roost. Someone who caves in to emotions, and brings negativity to the environment.

Put yourself into both sets of shoes for a few minutes. Feel what it is like to BE the person of character; to BE the person who has no power in change. In your mind's eye, draw out the effects on others. And think about what each stance creates.

You'll see that both your inner and the outer world depend more than you may have thought, on WHO you are—on your CHARACTER. And you'll see that character is a choice, not a given.

Part II Conclusion

WHO YOU ARE—your character—relates to your beliefs. Both are with you every minute of every day. There may be situations and circumstances where you do things that are out of character or that go against your beliefs (There may be major rewards or punishments that draw you away from your center!).

Actually, you can tell what the strength of your and another's character is by noticing what it takes to cause "uncharacteristic" actions!

Thanks to people who take stands, are aware of their beliefs, use their emotions to add heart and energy into what they do, and are committed to adding value in their world, humanity itself adds value to the complex web of life on this planet. And, thanks to these characteristics in YOU, change finds another steward who can test and nurture it—for the good of our businesses, communities, and governments, today and tomorrow.

How Empowering is Your Character?

A Questionnaire

Answer the following questions to help you assess your strength of character:

1. *Taking a Stand.* Pick the three things from the list below that are most important to you:

    -Achievement
    -Autonomy
    -Family
    -Financial security
    -Physical health
    -Impact
    -Influence
    -Loyalty
    -Personal growth
    -Recognition
    -Relationships
    -Security
    -Service
    -Other (add to the list)

    Rate yourself for each value: I am fully living this value (0=not at all, 1=rarely, 2=sometimes, 3=nearly always)

    Value #1: _____

    Value #2: _____

    Value #3:_____

What would you need to do or give up in order to live each value more fully? Is it worth the price?

2. *Self-Awareness.* How *aware* are you of your work-related beliefs? Here are some questions to help you get more in touch with the beliefs that influence your character:

-What do you believe is the proper relationship between managers and the people they lead?
-Who do you think is responsible for your career management? You? Management? The organization?
-What work events and people do you complain about to third parties? Are there any themes to the complaints?
-What work decisions did you make in the last month?
-What do your answers tell you about your assumptions and beliefs?

3. *Emotions as Motivators.* When did you last feel angry at work? What did you do?

-Erupt and increase tension between you and others?
-Stay quiet and feel bad, betrayed, or unappreciated?
-Use your anger to motivate a constructive action to solve the problem or let people know how you feel?

What is happening around you that might change your work or life? Do you see this as a threat or opportunity? How are you dealing with it?

How would you rate your use of your emotions as a constructive force in change?

0	1	2	3	4	5

I feel disconnected
from my emotions,
not in charge

I appreciate my
emotions and
feelings, try to
understand them

4. *Adding Value in Your World.*

-Would the people around you describe you as an optimist or pessimist? What impact do you think your attitudes have on others?

-What would you like your legacy to be to the world around you? What positive impact have you had so far?

-What exists today that wouldn't exist or be as positive without you?

Think of all the areas where you would like to have positive impact. How are you progressing in creating that legacy?

0	1	2	3	4	5
No or little progress					I am where I want to be in creating and adding value

PART III

Powerful Actions

ULTIMATELY, CHANGE IS ACTION. And effective action draws on skills and knowledge. Beliefs and character are necessary, but not sufficient to make things happen.

In this part, you'll explore four kinds of action that make you a strong player in the change business:

Be a Business
Develop Information Age Skills
Be Your Own Human Resource Manager
Take Charge of Your Own Change Process

Be a Business

WHAT DOES IT MEAN to BE a business? Here are some requirements and suggestions:

◈ A business *provides products, services, information* and various emotional benefits (like "peace of mind") in return for money, future commitments, more information, etc.

> *SUGGESTION:* know what products, services, information, and emotional benefits YOU, Inc. can and want to deliver right now and in the future. Know what these are worth in the marketplace. Sell yourself in terms of the value of what you DELIVER.

◈ A business *optimizes its productivity.* The best productivity happens when we minimize costs and maximize benefits to customers. The question is, "How can we keep our costs down, get the highest price, and provide the highest value for the customers' investments?"

> *SUGGESTION:* Find every way you can to eliminate the costs of being YOU, Inc. Are there reports that don't add value?

Approvals that are a waste of time? Steps in a process that delay things unnecessarily? People involved who don't add value? Things you do that can't be justified for either short- or long-term reasons? Get rid of everything that isn't necessary.

Then look at the "outputs" you deliver—the products and services you provide. Ask yourself how you could make them even more valuable to people who get them. (e.g., Do you help solve technical problems on the telephone? What if you kept a log of the kind of problems and sent it routinely to the engineering department? What if you called customers who were really irate to see how things are going?—thus increasing their loyalty to the organization). Try to find things to do that cost very little, yet have huge value to the receiver or customer.

◈ A business *sets goals and gets feedback.*

SUGGESTION: Take charge of what you will do, and how you will contribute. Manage your own feedback processes. You are not a victim in an economic web. You are a key and conscious player. Find out what people need and work with them to create your goals. Then, continuously find out how what you are delivering is being received and used. The "old world of work" expected managers to do this for you. Switch the rules around. Take charge of what you will do. Get your own feedback from people who get your work. Use feedback to help you do a better job and (of course) to help you feel appreciated.

Take charge of your job. Make it relevant. If you don't take charge someone else will, and your life and work will lose something in the process.

◈ A business *exists in networks*—of suppliers, customers, industries, governments, professions, and other communities of interest.

SUGGESTION: Draw a picture of YOU, Inc. as part of a network. Include people and groups you learn from, provide things to, receive things from. Include the organization you work for, but go outside its boundaries. Think of You, Inc., not your job in XYZ corporation, agency or foundation.

◈ A business *projects itself into the future.* It looks at emerging trends, needs, technologies, opportunities and challenges. It identifies what it can create for the future and is aware of what is getting obsolete.

SUGGESTION: Put yourself into arenas where you can think about and explore the future. Read, go to professional meetings, find out about global and competitive trends. If you are a full- or part-time employee somewhere, take a look at the organization's strategic plan. Imagine that YOU, Inc. is developing its strategy as a little business of One for the future. Have some fun with this as you look at options.

◈ A business is *aware of its core competencies*—and protects, develops, and nurtures them.

SUGGESTION: Do you know what your core competencies are? The knowledge and skills that are deeply rooted in you— that you love to and are committed to use? To find them, just ask yourself when you have felt most alive while working. Was it when you were solving tough technical problems? Helping others learn and develop? Negotiating tough deals? Leading complex change projects? These motivated competencies contain the seed of your future work, even if aspects of them may be getting obsolete. Make a list of your motivated competencies and figure out how to leverage them in the future.

◈ A business *blends short-term and long-term interests.* Successful businesses address both. They maximize the short-term and they feed the long-term. I consulted to the General Electric Company for many years. The company has several planning and review processes that are future-oriented. Everyone participates in them, every year. If a short-term dilemma interferes—well—it's addressed too. It's an ethic in the company. The ethic says, we will excel today AND we will prepare for and help create tomorrow. We will "bring good things to life," today AND tomorrow!

SUGGESTION: Sometimes when we look at how we'd like to spend our time today and what we want/need to do in the future, they don't easily fit together. It's like any business that has to keep itself functioning today AND prepare for the future. You may not be doing today what you want to do tomorrow. Yet you must keep bread on the table, live a life now. If your future goals are quite out of sync with today, then you have a challenging time ahead. Like any business that says, "we have to change," "YOU, Inc." may find yourself in a dual role: holding the fort today while also preparing for a new future.

YOU IN THE ECONOMIC WEB

Consider creating a YOU, Inc. that has a business ethic for yourself:

1. Know the products, services, and information you can deliver

2. Optimize your productivity

3. Set goals and get feedback

4. Cultivate a network where you can leverage yourself

5. Think about and prepare for the future

6. Know and develop your core competencies

7. Simultaneously manage short- and long-term interests and goals

If you can do these things, then you will become a successful business—you will BE a business in the future. You will be *YOU, Inc.!* whether you are a contractor, consultant, part-time employee, full-time employee, or economic web browser!

Develop Information Age Skills

IMAGINE WHAT IT WAS like for people to make the shift from hunting and gathering to an agricultural society (about 3500 B.C.). Imagine the new skills that nomadic people needed just to succeed in a community that stayed in one place and could begin to develop all the roles and processes we associate with a town.

Most likely, interpersonal skills and conflict management became increasingly more important. So did intellectual skills for developing laws and planning things. People started to need more awareness of soils and natural cycles, so they could sow, reap, and support birthing cycles of animals. These were different skills and knowledge than people needed when they were constantly moving, hunting, and protecting themselves from new enemies in new environments.

Now, imagine what it must have been like for our ancestors of the 1700s and 1800s, when steamers, the printing press, cotton gin, sewing machine, and other equipment of the industrial age emerged. Think about how different it was for the men (and children) to "go to work" in factories instead of at home. Imagine how land barons, who grew up with land-based wealth, must have felt when "upstart" people without aristocratic or gentrified backgrounds got rich from their industries. Think about the new skills needed to plan, organize, and control the big industrial operations of the last two hundred years. And imagine how society must have changed when money, not land, became the basis for social movement and organization.

Every major age has its critical skills and competencies. As we enter the Information Age, technology is doing more of the routine and dangerous work. Electronics are radically transforming communications, relationships, products, services, and even how we design and make things.

Are YOU ready to succeed in the new Information Age? Do you have the basic, foundation competencies this evolving world requires of you?

◈ Communicating, networking, relating

◈ Decision-making and problem-solving

◈ Thinking: creatively, systemically, critically

◈ Learning and teaching

◈ Financial and business knowledge

Communicating, Networking, Relating. Most work today requires us to work with others. As YOU, Inc., you can't be an island. None of us can. We have to work with others. And, in an age of speed and innovation, we have to debate, disagree, have conflicts, as well as dialogue with and listen to others. Fifteen years ago, Peter Krembs and I wrote a book called *On the Level: Communicating about Performance.* It focused on how to communicate in a two-way manner and across authority levels. It focused on the communication between managers and the people they led. Then six years ago, Peter and I revised it. The communication demands of the world had significantly shifted. The economic web had expanded. We expanded the book to include communications among suppliers, customers, management, unions, and workers.

One of the great communication challenges of our age is to be able to communicate with ANYONE—even our "boss" three levels up—as an equal player. We have to communicate in spite of differences in rank, authority, expertise, age, gender, race, economic status, and geographic location. For this, we need better and better communication skills. Conflict is not bad. Debate is not bad. Both can add a lot of value if they happen in an environment of trust and creative thinking. We have to learn how to communicate in these situations without destroying the "adversary."

Decision-Making and Problem-Solving. Everyone makes decisions. Everyone solves problems. A person who sweeps the floor decides how to deal with problems due to rain, spills, etc. Someone who leads a large organization decides what direction to go for the future.

The first realization is that EVERYONE is a decision-maker and problem-solver. When you realize that you are in the middle of a problem or decision, then you need Information Age skills for success. These include:

◈ *Recognizing that there is a decision to make or a problem to solve.* I have interviewed many executives and entrepreneurs. An astounding finding: they often don't realize they are making a decision or solving a problem. They just act and move on.

◈ *Deciding HOW to make the decision or solve the problem.* A decision or problem solution has two parts: 1) deciding what to do, and 2) getting it done. The decision isn't made or the problem solved until both parts happen.

If you must make a decision or solve a problem, always ask yourself, "Who needs to be involved in order for us to have the best decision/solution?" AND "Who needs to be involved in order for us to have a successful implementation of the solution or decision?"

Based on your answers to these questions, you can decide whom to involve in solving the problem or making the decision. You have lots of options. You can make the decision yourself and then discuss it with others. You can consult with others, but make it yourself; you can get others involved in a consensus decision (everyone has to agree to the decision or at least agree to actively support it), or you can delegate it to others/someone else.

It takes a special skill and knowledge to manage decision-making and problem-solving this way. But it is important for everyone to have this ability!

Thinking: Critically, Creatively, Systemically. Think of all the interesting challenges that go with "taking a stand," "knowing your own assumptions," "using your emotions," "adding value in your world." These all require a new level of consciousness from all of us.

And that new consciousness places new demands on how we think. Formal education may have helped us learn how to find, memorize, and analyze information.

But today's world, first of all, asks us to think more *critically*. With information coming from so many places and perspectives, we have to be both open and skeptical. Is what we have just heard *the truth*? Is there good evidence for it? Is the source of the information credible? Do the conclusions make sense? We have to hone our *critical thinking skills* so that we aren't duped and misled.

Second, as machines take over more of the routine work, the value we add is increasingly *creative* value. We come up with new designs, figure out ways to better solve problems and meet needs, find ways to reduce costs, and discover changes to products and services. But all of these require different ways of thinking. We've got to be able to get out of old thought boxes by using lateral and metaphorical thinking (e.g., "How can we make the new train perform like a sled on ice?"). This kind of thinking draws on different parts of the brain than rational and analytical methods! People who tap into this "right side of the brain" will have advantage in the future. Will you?

Third, we need to think more *systemically*. Everything we do today has direct and indirect effects. We don't want to get too tangled up in all of the implications of what we do, but we all need to think beyond the immediate cause and effects. The goal, of course, is to make sure that what we do and decide today has positive direct and indirect results both today and tomorrow, here and there. We want to avoid actions that seem positive today but create havoc in the future—or are good for us "here," but not for others "there."

When we think about things *systemically*, we may even decide to do something that seems negative in the short term in order to get great benefits in the long term (like restrict certain foods today in order to be healthier tomorrow, or work hard on an initially unprofitable new idea in order to have a hit in the future). Of course, it's nice to do things that are positive in the short and long term, and both here and there.

Fortunately, we all have the ability to increase our *critical, creative, and systemic* thinking skills. Those who do it have a decisive advantage in these times of accelerating change.

Learning and Teaching. When I went to school, there was a clear distinction between learning and working. I was supposed to go to school for 12, 16, 20 years and then work. The model is different today. If we don't continue to learn, our knowledge gets old—fast. Virtually every field of human knowledge is going through a big transformation today—often shaken at its very foundation. This is true in all the sciences, in management, and in the arts. The reason is that information acts on itself. When there is a little of it, new ideas come slowly—with periodic breakthroughs. When there is twice as much, new ideas increase *exponentially*—double the information and you will quadruple the implications!!

This has a big lesson for all of us: be prepared to keep on learning. This means being able to listen, read, extract information from media. It means being able to have conversations in order to learn, to watch others in order to learn, to learn by trying things out on your own, and learn by noticing and tracking mistakes and successes.

It also means that all of us teach. Even if we aren't conscious of it, others watch and learn from us. New people come to work or into the family—and we have a chance to influence their learning. The question is, "Will you be a great teacher and helper?" Will you be able to help others focus on important things to learn? Help them feel confident that they can develop new knowledge and skills? Support them in hard times? Be a sounding board? These are all important skills that all of us can bring to each other.

Develop Your Financial and Business Capacity. In the mid-90s, the American Society for Quality surveyed several hundred middle and upper managers from large corporations. There were ten questions on the survey—questions about the financial and economic basics of a business (e.g., "True or False: The net worth of a business is the amount of cash it possesses"). The average number of correct answers (out of ten) was three!!

Sadly, many people don't really understand the economics of a business. They have trouble seeing the need for profit, the implications of investment, the costs of adding full-time people to the payroll, the trade-offs between meeting the shareholders' quarterly expectations and delaying a key strategic project.

I first found, working to increase participation levels in South African businesses, that people couldn't participate effectively without some financial knowledge. In fact, even today I recommend that "economics basics" be part of any organization's shift to more participative governance. And (recall the poor management scores on the financial survey), people at all levels and in all roles often need development in this area.

Are you ready with these Information Age skills? Are your communication, problem-solving and decision-making, thinking, learning and teaching, and financial competencies up to snuff for these changing times? Don't worry if you feel like you're playing catch-up. We all are. These are life skills, after all. We'll be building and honing them for the rest of our lives.

INFORMATION AGE SKILLS

Be Your Own Human Resource Manager

MANY BIG ORGANIZATIONS CAME OUT of the Industrial Age having done people a great disservice. They tried to "take care" of employees: make "human resource" decisions about their development, careers, work content and location. They perpetuated a myth of dependency ("We will decide what you do and where you go.") And many of us colluded in the myth!

When we expose this myth, it horrifies us. Yet many organizations and people today continue to operate in this dependent way. It's time for all of us to stop conceding our powers to others and take charge of ourselves in work and life.

Being your own human resource manager is part of being a key and powerful player in the economic web. This doesn't mean you should defy the business and leaders; it's important to add value and to align your energies with larger goals. It does mean that YOU, as CEO of YOU, Inc., have the right and responsibility to play a significant role in managing your own development, career, and work.

If you work for an organization, it's in their best interest to help you do this. But it's your life and career. You can use your knowledge

and skills in many places in the economic web. You are not a pawn in the organization—and will actually increase your value there by taking care of yourself. Specifically, you can:
-Have clear performance goals
-Go after the work that uses your motivated competencies
-Find out what your competencies are worth
-Have a vision of your future
-Develop networks
-Have an active learning agenda

Have Clear Performance Goals

Right now in your organization, things work in a certain way. Things work the way they do because an array of forces and conditions support them as the *status quo*. These same forces and conditions make change difficult. Goals and objectives you set for yourself can provide a counterforce to the status quo. They are especially important when you want to implement or influence changes. Goals tell you what you want to accomplish. They help you envision a new state of things. Through this, they help motivate and guide change even when the local conditions don't support it.

Many (but certainly not all) organizations require that their people have and document performance goals or objectives. In some cases, the manager or "boss" decides what these are. In other cases, you and your manager might work together to define what you will deliver in your job. In a few rare cases, customers may even be involved in helping set individual goals. If your organization has a process for setting performance goals, that's great. If it doesn't, then you must do it on your own.

The important thing is to see performance goals as YOUR TOOL for managing yourself and change. As the rabbit in Alice in Wonderland remarked, "If you don't know where you are going, any road will get you there!" Goals help you prioritize your actions and direct your energy. They keep you from falling into the crisis trap, where you just react to things as they happen, whether or not they are important. Goals also give you perspective on the smaller and often unrewarding actions you need to take in order to be successful. Metaphorically, knowing that you are walking to a friend's house gives meaning and direction to the steps you take.

If you develop them with others, performance goals can help increase your influence and support in the organization. When other people collaborate in setting them, they become collaborators in your success. Also, when you negotiate and talk about your goals with others, it's less likely that you'll hear, "But I thought you were going to . . ." It's more likely that you will get support. Think specifically about talking about your goals with the people who *receive* your work. Discover what they need and want—how they will evaluate what they get. Doing this leads you to creating more value in your work.

See yourself as a business-within-a-business. Know what you are going to accomplish—and be sure that the key people who are affected by or who will evaluate your work share your sense of direction and results. Don't wait for others to do this. And, don't treat goal-setting as a game or a bureaucratic process—even though others may approach it that way. Turn the goal-setting process into your own personal self-management tool. Take charge of the process for yourself. Use it to help you thrive in and influence change—to make a difference at work.

Go After the Work That Uses Your Motivated Competencies

Where there is energy, there is action. Where there is energy for work, there is also joy. Do everything you can to match your work and your energy. One way to think about this relates to "motivated competencies." Think about times in the past, whether at work or in other settings, where you were doing things and feeling alive and competent. Describe these times in writing. Then, list the knowledge, skills and values you were using in those situations. Think about the technical knowledge you used, the interpersonal skills, the thinking skills, the kind of end result you helped to achieve. Note whether you were happiest when doing these things alone or with others, whether the rewards were external or inside you. Consider the list you are making to be your "motivated competencies."

In your own words, create a checklist of your motivated competencies, and use it to evaluate your current job. Then look around you at work. Are there parts of your job that you want to do more of? Are there projects or other jobs that might better fit your motivated competencies? Are there teams you could join where the work would be more of a match for your talents and interests? Are there any parts of your current job that are not a good fit for you? If so, is there a way to pass them on to anyone else?

Every job has parts that fit you and parts that don't. You'll be a more powerful player in change if you try to get more parts that fit, while either removing or repositioning parts that don't. For example, for those parts that don't use your motivated competencies, try to make a game of them (when I peeled potatoes years ago, I always tried to beat my previous record of potatoes per hour), or come up with innovations. You can also contact the people who receive the parts you least prefer and reconnect with the importance of these parts to them.

Another very powerful tactic is to discover the deeper meaning of your less-preferred work. I've worked with janitors who, when they focused on the value they added to the image of the company and the safety of the customers, found greater meaning in sweeping the floors. I've worked with coal miners deep in the earth who in severe work conditions found meaning in the fact that "I get the coal out," and "I am the only human being who ever sat on this piece of earth." Then there are the semi-literate gardeners in South Africa who discovered that they directed more people to the right offices than did the receptionist. They'd never appreciated the value of that part of their job. For managers who hate giving performance feedback, the energizing reason might be "helping someone get better," or "making sure the technical project succeeds."

The point is, set up your job for high energy. Go after projects and jobs that use your motivated competencies. Search for the deeper importance—related to your values and interests—of those job parts that don't fit your energy and competence profile. If you can, find ways to pass on parts of your work that don't draw on your strengths or tap into your energy.

Never allow yourself to be a pawn in the institutional world. You have many freedoms, many choices, and many ways that you can shape your job, today or tomorrow, to contribute to a good life for you and to success for your organization. Sure, it's easy to feel powerless and dependent. But, as many very successful people have found, the forces that keep us down are often more imagined than real.

I remember working with executives from both the public and private sectors who would swap jobs for several months. These were very high potential people—on the track to major leadership positions. Interviews found one common success factor. They "assumed consent." This means that they took what they thought were the right actions without asking permission. They did this even when it wasn't "by the book." Most of the time they didn't meet any resistance. Their actions prevailed. This is not a recommendation to defy your organization. On the contrary, action without responsibility is recklessness. But, it is a call to bring your best to your work, for the organization and for yourself.

Find Out What Your Competencies are Worth

There is a big shift going on in the employment world. It is often called the shift to "free agency." This refers to a big change in the employment contract. We can no longer expect to work for an employer for life, nor can an employer expect a worker to commit to the organization for life. Some people think this means that people are disposable. It really means that we face a new kind of exchange. "I will give the organization my skills and energy for immediate results. In return, I expect fair pay and good working conditions." "I will help position the organization for success in the future. In return I expect some kind of investment in my future—in the form of retirement benefits or personal development."

It's important to be clear about the value exchange between you and your organization. A key part of this exchange relates to your competencies: your knowledge, skills, and values. These are assets for the organization. Your pay reflects the organization's valuation of these assets. You can only be a powerful player in change if you know the value, in the larger market, of the competencies you bring. Yet few people know what the value of their competencies is on the open market.

Discover your competencies' value by looking at the employment ads in your area. Find out by listing with electronic employment services. Find out by talking with people in other organizations. The reason for doing this is not to quit your job. It is not to negotiate a higher wage. It is to find out the value of your competencies in the world at large. When you know the value of what you bring, you can be a much more powerful and assertive player in change. You can have greater confidence in your voice and ideas.

It doesn't benefit you or your organization for you to feel small and unimportant. It's also negative if you overestimate the value of what you bring. Neither too big, nor too small is an appropriate valuing of your competencies. "Just right" is the key. Know what your competencies are worth. See your value in your workplace. Manage and influence change from that place. If you find that you are underpaid and undervalued, make a business case to appreciate or better use your skills. If that doesn't work, find a place that will value what you offer. Knowing that you have the option to leave will unleash a lot of energy for change if you decide to stay. This is the meaning of opening the bird's cage door. She can leave if she wants to, but sings ever more brightly if the choice is to stay. I know the truth of this from a manager's and business owner's perspective. The greatest loyalty is founded in choice.

Have a Vision of Your Future

Change is interesting for many reasons. But how we view it depends on how we view time. If we only lived in the present, with no past or future, then change would not be an issue, for we wouldn't recognize it as change. Living totally in the *present* is only an option for people who have lost all of their ability to remember. For people who think mainly about the *past,* change is often a disturbing and frightening thing. When we add a *future* dimension and see life and work as unfolding events and opportunities, then change is less scary. For this reason, it is important, from time to time, to think about ourselves in a variety of future scenarios.

You can get out ahead of change by thinking about the future. Then, it can't come as a total surprise or trigger extreme backlash and trauma. This is true whether your vision of the future is "accurate" or not. The key is to accept that the future will be different—to see this as normal.

So look at all the forces at play today that could become big jolts in YOUR future. Think about the forces that could have a really negative effect . . . a positive effect on your work and life. If you can, open yourself up to others' views of the future. Read some of the articles about your industry and profession, especially the ones that speculate about what's to come.

Imagine yourself in this changing world in one year, two years, five years, and beyond. What conditions around you do you think will be different? How would you like those years to look and be and feel? What skills, knowledge and values would you like to be using? What kind of work do you want to do? Have big dreams, but know that if they are extraordinarily big, you will need extraordinary energy to make them come alive. Keep your dreams high, but within your reach, building on the motivated competencies you've developed over the years.

Behind all these questions is one that drives them all: What is your purpose in life: why are you here? When you link the answer to this question with your work, when you envision your future work as a way of living your purpose, then you will be a member of a very elite corps. You will see change as a part of life—of your life. And, from that perspective, you will be a powerful player in change and life, wherever you are.

Develop Networks

People who are disconnected from others often find themselves in dead ends. They have a really tough time dealing with change because they face it alone. We are not meant to face change alone. The workplace is a social system. It is a network of relationships and conversations. Any change affects everyone in some way. But, we need to see ourselves in the network—with fellow sojourners. When we see ourselves this way we increase our options. We expand our sources of learning and support. Change becomes "our" not "my" challenge. We feel that we don't have to do things alone, that we are in this together.

When we are connected with others, we often get early warning signals about change—advance notice of challenges, new ideas, trends. We can also tap into others' energies and visions.

When we are trusted by and trust others in a broader network, we often find ourselves with more options. A project starts, and someone who knows your interests and skills recommends you for the team. A job opens, and someone proposes you as a candidate. A traumatic downsizing occurs, and colleagues in the network begin to help with a job search. A change begins, and someone in another department suggests that you should be consulted for implementation ideas.

None of these things can happen unless people know you personally, trust you and value you. This requires an investment of time and energy to develop relationships and communicate about what you can and want to do.

Make a list of 10-20 people who you want to be associated with, who can influence decisions about your career or who have information and perspectives that can help you thrive in the future. Call them, talk to them. Take them out for coffee and tell them about yourself. Ask about them. Think about where people you can learn from and who can help your work and career, hang out. Go to association meetings. Get involved in projects that give you exposure. Do what you can to become a vibrant player in the larger idea and influence net.

Have an Active Learning Agenda

We learn all the time. Learning goes with life—it is life. And learning takes many forms. Sometimes we plan it, sometimes we don't. But the point is that learning is the great process of life. It is growth and the creative energy expressing itself through our curiosity and questions, our confusions, and our solution-oriented approach to the variety of life and work puzzles we face.

Since learning is a natural part of life. It doesn't require a lot of planning and consciousness. But when we apply consciousness and planning to learning, amazing things can happen. People learn new skills and embark on new careers. They plan to overcome speech anxiety and, through practice and sheer will, begin to stir audiences to action. They finish high school, go on to college and even get PhD's after middle age. They start small businesses and get coaching from financial and marketing experts—creating new employment opportunities for others.

On a smaller—but no less important scale—people learn new methods, procedures, skills that help them do their jobs better. They practice and persist until they get it right. They take classes, read, do self-study, find webinars and e-learning classes.

You are part of this learning web. Resources and support are everywhere. Be bold in choosing what you want to learn, and dogged in pursuing it and getting it right for you. As long as you are learning, there is life. And when your learning is deliberate and chosen, you are more likely to be the master of your fate.

In many larger organizations, there is a Human Resource or Personnel Department to design and manage these processes. If the processes work, by all means use them. But put yourself in the driver's seat. Don't hand your management of yourself over to anyone—not to

BE YOUR OWN HUMAN RESOURCE MANAGER

HR, not to management—not to anyone else. Get the agreements and support you need from others, but manage your own job design, your own goals, your own feedback, your own learning, your own career, your own selection and recruiting process. While you may not get your own way, you'll be a person of power and consciousness in the organization. And you'll help create a new culture of personal responsibility and empowerment.

Take Charge of Your Own Change Process

THINK AGAIN OF THE kinds of changes we all face in life. Some are irreversible, like growing old. Some occur around us because other people make decisions, like setting out to reorganize a business. Still others happen because natural shifts occur—children leave home, new projects we are working on get old and have to be replaced, we get older and have to change some of our living patterns. And, of course, we often make decisions to change—to marry, to move to a new place, to change our work or job.

All of these shifts, even the voluntary ones, cause feelings of uncertainty and anxiety. For years, psychologists have talked about our reactions to change as a holdover from the Stone Age—when people faced constant threat from animals and the elements. "We were programmed then," they say, "to *fight and defend, flee, or freeze and comply.*"

Today, probably the most common response is compliance. It's not like the Stone Age days when our ancestors faced life-threatening dangers and had to fight. So, many people resort to compliance. They give in, believing that they simply have no choice. They opt for a slow death of the spirit rather than defending or running away. Maybe today we should be seeing more of the latter two responses in situations where changes really are threatening to our spirits and the institutions we live and work in!

There are several additional and more sophisticated ways to think about change. Knowing about them may help you be *more aware* of what is happening when you face changes. Then you will hopefully be more patient with yourself, less likely to unconsciously *defend and fight, flee, or freeze and comply*. Perhaps knowing them will help you be more courageous in taking charge of and moving with your own change process.

The Grief Cycle. In the 60s, Elizabeth Kubler-Ross, a psychotherapist, noticed that dying people, and people who had lost a loved one, went through a common cycle of reactions as they dealt with death. Later, she discovered that any significant loss (loss of a job, a child leaving home, even the loss of an important project at work or a loss of a familiar work environment or structure) triggered these reactions.

◈ First, we *deny* the change ("He is not really dead," "The marriage isn't really over," "This change is just a fad; it won't last").

◈ Then we move to *anger and blame.* We strike out in some way (talk about evil motives of people in charge, sabotage the changes, refuse to cooperate, try to find allies and resist).

◈ Third, we try to *bargain* ("God, I'll change myself if you just bring her back," "If we just work harder, maybe they'll decide not to sell our part of the company").

◈ Fourth, we often go into a time of *sadness, depression.* We slow down and lose motivation.

◈ Then we either *stay stuck* or we *accept* that change is happening, begin to look to the future, examine what we have to do to participate, and move ahead. We learn, and get on with our lives under new conditions.

Think about any big change you have experienced. You'll probably find that you cycled through these phases (denial, anger, bargaining, depression, acceptance and renewal). You may also find, as many have, that it's important to let yourself go through these stages. People who don't—who don't let themselves feel their emotions—usually find that

GRIEF CYCLE

they either become very bitter or that they can never fully let go of a past that is really gone. They also find that the next time they have a loss, it is harder to move on.

Why? Because any new loss opens up the unresolved grief of the past. Psychologists make an important point about this. They say it is important to "burn your wood." That is, to let yourself fully deal with every change and loss. Or else the unburned wood will make the next fire bigger. In a time where change is such a common thing, none of us can afford to save up for a big bonfire!

I have also found—as many people have—that it is very useful to *know* the grief cycle stages. Then I don't feel "abnormal" when I find myself in the cycle (although I certainly feel the anguish of the stages!).

The Hero's/Heroine's Journey. Every one of us is on a life journey. In fact, there are powerful forces propelling us forward through a variety of life stages. We know that our intellectual and emotional capacity can keep developing through our life. We are "wired" for that to happen.

But we have choices. We can be an ally in our own development. We can be neutral. Or we can be our own adversary. Mythologist and

philosopher, Joseph Campbell, spent his life studying what happens as
we make these choices. He believed, as do many psychologists, that
myth and stories reflect deep truths about us as human beings. Here
are some of the conclusions he came to after studying myth and stories
from all over the world:

⬥ We have two broad choices in life. We can follow the "right-
hand path," where we seek stability and follow rules without
question. Or we can follow our "bliss," living a creative life,
moving into danger, trying to bring forth something new.

⬥ If we choose the second alternative, then we take "the hero's or
heroine's journey." On this journey we do things like:

• See changes that are occurring as a *"call to adventure,"* a challenge to look at things in a different way and to explore—
perhaps, as in the old fairy tales, to "go into the dark forest"
or, like Odysseus, to sail into the unknown.

• *Accept help* if it's available. In the myths and fairy tales, there
are gods and goddesses (the goddess Athena helped
Odysseus), fairy godmothers (remember Cinderella), and
wise advisors (Merlin) who may come in disguise.

• *Meet challenges and trials in places where we have no or little
control*—and may even be threatened (remember the story of
Jonah in the belly of the whale? Of Christ in the tomb? Of
Buddha outside the palace gates? Numerous folk and fairy
tales about sleeping princesses and lost children? Of the
caterpillar in the cocoon?).

All significant learning demands that we go into an uncertain time
and space. The only way we really learn and grow is to enter the
unknown, lose control, and stretch ourselves—try new things.
Think about any adventure story you have ever read, and you will
know that uncertainty, trials, and tests shape and strengthen us, and
open us up to new areas of life.

⬥ Learn how to *responsibly use power*. This is probably the biggest
lesson of all myth. Each of us has power (even more today, since
all it takes is one person to infect the world's computers with
viruses). The heroes and heroines in myth must find and earn
their power. They have to meet the great tests. They must show

a balance of good heart and wise mind. When they do, they move into new arenas: Cinderella to the castle, Odysseus to his kingship . . . .

◈ *Bring personal lessons to others.* It's one thing to learn something yourself. It's quite another to bring what you learn to others. One interesting challenge we face when we let ourselves take the hero's/heroine's journey is, "Am I willing to bring what I learned to others? Do I have the energy, commitment, and even the guts to do it?" Some choose not to. They don't go that last step of the journey.

Mainstream / Marginalized Journey. I must add a wrinkle to the Hero/Heroine's Journey. There are different ways the journey unfolds, depending on whether you are a member of the group who has institutional or social power (the mainstream) or are a member of a group that doesn't have easy access to privileges (a marginalized group). Gender, race, education, background and social status—these all influence

THE HERO/HEROINE JOURNEY

whether you are more insider or outsider. They all influence whether it is relatively easy or difficult to get formal leadership positions.

The challenge for those who are members of the "mainstream" group is to *become worthy of the power they are born into.* That, in fact, is the story of Odysseus, one of the original mythic heroes. He was born to be king. But he had to *earn* his moral right to be king. That is what the Odyssey is about!

People who are members of the more "marginalized" group—who weren't "born to be king"—have a different challenge and take a different journey. They often first try to do things the way the "mainstream group" does them. For example, a woman may become very rational and authoritarian in order to succeed in the organization. She may get to a high position—be successful because she is "like a traditional male leader." But, as many women today are feeling, she loses herself. She gets stressed (women worldwide are more stressed than men), and feels like an alien. Often, she will leave the organization where the pressures are to take a hardened version of the "hero's journey" and to become a more traditional kind of leader somewhere else. She then rediscovers her feminine side—her nurturing, intuitive, communal side—and tries to find ways to marry it with her well-developed authoritarian skills (those that helped her be successful earlier on).

MAINSTREAM/MARGINALIZED PATHS

The same is true for people of other "marginalized" groups: races, ages, etc. Heroes (masculine, and in the West, white/mainstream) are called on, more than ever, to open the door to diversity—to integrate "marginalized" values and views into their own actions, life, and consciousness. The great heroes of today are champions of broader thinking and sensitivities. As Franklin Delano Roosevelt said, "no one is free until everyone is free." And the essence of freedom is the ability to participate in and influence change.

As we enter the next part of the Information Age, integrating all voices will become increasingly important. As we deal with the specific changes happening in our day-to-day work and life, we have an exciting challenge to see them as part of the framework of the larger change that is happening all over the world.

At the end of the day, for each of us personally, it doesn't matter whether we are part of the "mainstream" or "marginalized" groups. The challenge is equally there and exciting, even though the issues each group faces may be different. For the hero/heroine journey is more than your personal change process and challenge. We are all living it: male or female, rich or poor, black or white, life calls us to participate in change. As Campbell says, we are all called to adventure. It's terribly sad when we let misunderstood fears, or the fears of others, get in the way of our own living.

Part III Conclusion

WHILE NONE OF US can control the world around us, we can take charge of or at least understand ourselves in change. For this it helps to understand the psychology of change, the role of change in our lives, and the actions we can take to ensure our own sanity and effectiveness in the often-turbulent times around us.

There are four powerful actions to take in order to get these benefits:

Be a business. See yourself as YOU, Inc., a little business with capabilities and with products and services to sell.

Develop Information Age skills. Sharpen your communication, problem-solving and decision-making, thinking, learning and teaching, and financial capabilities.

Be your own human resource manager. Get support and information, but don't rely on others to manage you, your development, your job searches, your team assignments, your career.

Take charge of change. Be aware of the very special dynamics of change and use this awareness to help you react sensitively and effectively.

Remember, *Change is EVERYBODY'S Business.* It is *YOUR business!!*

How Empowered are Your Actions?

A Questionnaire

Here is a list of the skills from Part III ("Powerful Actions"). Rate each as follows:

> 1=Major weakness
> 2=Minor weakness
> 3=Neither a strength nor weakness
> 4=Moderate strength
> 5=Major strength

Section A: Be a Business

_____ 1. I know the products, services, and information I can deliver.

_____ 2. I am very productive, constantly eliminating irrelevant work.

_____ 3. I regularly set goals and get feedback from people who get my work.

_____ 4. I have strong networks that help me get work done and solve problems.

_____ 5. I take time to think about and prepare for the future.

_____ 6. I know and continually develop my core competencies.

_____ 7. I simultaneously focus on short- and long-term interests and goals.

Section B: Develop Information Age Skills

____   8.   I work with others in a way that builds relationships and creates open, two-way exchanges of ideas and information.

____   9.   I am adept at solving problems and making decisions.

____   10.   I use effective thinking techniques for different situations: critical, creative, and systemic (big picture) thinking.

____   11.   I am an effective learner and teacher, using and sharing knowledge, skills, and personal qualities.

____   12.   I understand business basics and can interpret financial information.

Section C: Be Your Own Human Resource Manager

____   13.   I am clear about and actively focused on my commitments.

____   14.   I do regular reviews of my knowledge and skills and forecasts of the knowledge and skills I'll need and want in the future.

____   15.   I know what my skills are worth in the marketplace.

____   16.   I read and talk about trends. I think about how changes ahead may affect me and my future.

____   17.   I actively cultivate networks of people who can support me and my work and future.

____   18.   I have an active learning agenda, knowing what I am trying to learn and what resources I'll use for that learning. Even if it's only 10 minutes a day, I find time to expand my boundaries.

Section D: Take Charge of Change

_____   19.   When I feel like running away or being defensive, I am able to stand back and put the situation in perspective so I can act constructively.

_____   20.   I constructively express and feel emotions when I lose something important to me. I give myself time to adjust to big changes.

_____   21.   I support others as they go through change.

_____   22.   I get and use the support of mentors and advisors.

_____   23.   When I am in a privileged or powerful position, I get everybody involved and committed.

_____   24.   When I am in a minority, I use constructive methods for getting my ideas heard.

_____   25.   I understand the dynamics of personal change and I recognize various change stages in myself and others.

Go back over your list.

Pick one strength (a 4 or 5) and one weakness (a 1 or 2) from each section:

	Strength	*Weakness*
A. Be a Business	_____	_____
B. Develop Information Age Skills	_____	_____
C. Be Your Own HR Manager	_____	_____
D. Take Charge of Change	_____	_____

◈ What conclusions can you draw about your change capabilities?

◈ Where are your major strengths? Weaknesses?

◈ What strengths can you leverage—use for greater benefit?

◈ What areas would you like to develop?

Afterword

TODAY, IN THE 21ST century, *Change is EVERYBODY's Business.* Ironically, at the very time when most of us feel so small, so disempowered, we can actually make more difference than ever. Information technology and the rise of democracy as the main form of governance are partly responsible for this new power of the individual.

Think about the power of one individual to launch a computer virus that disrupts business around the world. Or consider the outspoken stockholder at a televised shareholder meeting.

On a smaller scale, take any change that has happened in your workplace or other parts of your life. You will be able to track it back to a few people who wanted to make something different happen.

And for the changes around you that have not been "for the better," ask yourself what one courageous voice—yours—might have done to stop or reshape it.

Every day, each of us is called on to take a stand—to follow something new, support something old, come up with a new idea, react to a change or opportunity. Our initial reaction is often to resist or defend. This is because any reaction other than habit takes energy and conscious thought. It's easier to react in an automatic way, or to leave the response to others whose job it is to lead or to take action.

Reacting in automatic and habitual ways, resisting change, and letting others take responsibility for change may be appropriate in some situations. Resistance, for one thing, is sometimes a constructive response. But when we spend too much of our time reacting, we lose a lot of what is special about being human.

As human beings, we are able to be agents and initiators of change. We can accelerate trends and movements that we believe in. We can make a difference for our own lives and work and for those around us.

All of this requires a *belief* structure that supports empowered action. It relies on *character* qualities that help us act with courage. And, if we know *actions* and techniques for successful participation in change, we can be involved effectively when the time comes.

The ideas and assessments in this book are here to support you in committing to an empowered belief structure, building a courageous character for change, and adopting actions for participating in changes around you. If you skipped over the assessments, I urge you to go back and use them to help you take stock and develop helpful insights for the future. If you did complete them, take some time to review and think about what your responses mean for the future.

Whether in your workplace, your family, or other parts of your life, remember that change is not something out there that others own—

Change Is EVERYBODY's business!! Change is YOUR business!

Resources for Continued Learning

This book is a product of many experiences and resources. It draws on insights from the following recent *and* classic books:

Futurism. This area focuses on trends, scenarios, projections, hopes, and insights related to the future. It also examines ways that individuals, groups and communities prepare for the future.

Some interesting resources as we move into the 21st century include:

> Davis, S., & Meyer, C., *BLUR: The Speed of Change in the Connected Economy*. Boston: Addison-Wesley, 1998.

> Peck, S., *A World Waiting to Be Born: Civility Rediscovered*. New York: Bantam, 1993.

> Toffler, A., *Powershift: Knowledge, Wealth, and Violence at the Edge of the 21st Century*. New York: Bantam, 1991.

Mythology. It is clear that myths and fairy tales tell us a lot about how we unfold and change and grow. They reflect many of the greater truths of human nature. Myths also seem to change to capture the spirit or reflect the needs of the times. Joseph Campbell, a 20th century expert on myth said that myths simultaneously reflect a view of the world and the concerns and challenges of specific societies. They also provide teachings that guide us through life.

There are some wonderful books on mythology to increase your awareness of the role of myth in your life. I recommend that you read both about the "hero's" and the "heroine's" journeys. In some way they reflect the differences between mainstream and marginalized groups' specific change challenges.

> Campbell, J., *The Hero with a Thousand Faces*. Princeton: Princeton University Publications, 1972.

> Murdoch, E., *The Heroine's Journey*. Boston: Shambhala Pub., 1990.

> Pinkola-Estes, C., *Women Who Run with the Wolves*. New York: Ballentine Books, 1997.

The New Science. Physics, biology, chemistry, all the natural and physical sciences have been going through a massive transformation in this century. Some of the key shifts in thinking that influence this book are:

◈ While there are clearly general rules that govern nature, we will never be able to accurately predict any event that occurs in the living world.

◈ Everything in the universe is powerful. Everything exerts a gravitational force on everything else. Also, any particle, wave, or event can—given the right conditions—cause massive changes in the future.

◈ Life is NOT a chance event. The universe actually works in a way that seems to make life inevitable. The form (e.g., human) may not be inevitable, but, increasing *complexity* of forms DOES appear to be inevitable. The universe appears to be set up to become both more complex and more conscious.

◈ Collaboration is a key dynamic of evolution. Species do compete in order to strengthen themselves. But, in general, plants, animals, and the atmosphere work together to make life possible.

◈ Nothing is an island. Every particle, every human, every organization, is partly defined by other particles, humans, organizations. Individuals and organizations are who they are because of others as well as themselves.

◈ Major changes that occur in any organism are first discovered at the edges. That is, whatever part is closest to the environment is frequently the first to sense the need to change. This may be the skin on a body, a salesperson or a service person in a company. Executive and control functions (like a person's brain; the leadership team in an organization) are often the last to know about major problems or challenges at the edges.

◈ Every organism has a powerful ability to *self-organize*. This means that, if people in an organization realize that there is a need to change, they will rally quickly and spontaneously to do new things. They don't have to, and often won't, wait for the executives in the organization to direct things.

If you are interested in learning more—and willing to do heavy but fascinating reading, try some of these:

Capra, F., *The Web of Life: A New Understanding of the Web of Life.* London: Flamingo, 1997.

Kaufman, S., *The Search for Laws of Self-Organization and Complexity.* London: Oxford U Press, 1995.

Kelly, K., *New Rules for the New Economy: 10 Radical Strategies for a Connected World.* New York: Penguin, 1999.

Mindell, A., *The Quantum Mind: The Edge Between Physics and Psychology.* Portland: Lao Tse Press, 2000.

Ridley, M., *Genome.* New York: Harper Collins, 2000.

Wheatley, M., *Leadership and the New Science: Discovering Order in a Chaotic World, 2nd edition.* San Francisco: Berrett-Koehler, 2000.

Organization Development. OD is a discipline that focuses on change that supports increased organization capacity and health. Like Process Oriented Psychology (see below), it focuses on relationships, open expression, and increasing awareness. It adds a concern for institutional leadership, structures, systems, technology, and business processes that facilitate performance and change.

For further insights read:

Argyris, C., *Knowledge for Action: A Guide for Overcoming Barriers to Organization Change.* San Francisco: Jossey-Bass, 1993.

Bellman, G., *The Beauty of the Beast: Breathing New Life into Organizations.* San Francisco: Berrett-Koehler, 2000.

Block, P., *Stewardship: Choosing Service Over Self-Interest.* San Francisco: Berrett-Koehler, 1993.

McLagan, P., & Nel, C., *The Age of Participation: New Governance for the Workplace and the World.* San Francisco: Berrett-Koehler, 1996.

Personal Empowerment and Change. Some books provide direct action advice for individuals regarding taking charge of work, life, and careers. A few great resources include:

Covey, S., *First Things First.* New York: Simon & Schuster, 1994.

Fritz, R., *The Path of Least Resistance: Learning to Become the Creative Force in Your Own Life.* New York: Fawcett, 1989.

Jamison, K., *The Nibble Theory and the Kernel of Power.* New Jersey: Paulist Press, 1989.

McLagan, P. & Krembs, P., *On the Level: Performance Communication that Works.* San Francisco: Berrett-Koehler, 1996.

Moore, T., *The Re-Enchantment of Everyday Life.* New York: Harper Collins, 1996.

Reiss, G., *Changing Ourselves, Changing the World.* Tempe: New Falcon Publications, 2000.

White, R., *Living an Extraordinary Life.* Denver: ARCWorldwide, 2000.

Whiteley, R., *Love the Work You're With.* New York: Henry Holt, 2001.

Policy Science and Governance. This area examines ideas of community, leadership/followership, and the impact of values, assumptions, policies, and traditions on how organizations and communities operate. If you are interested in this area, read:

Etzioni, A., *Collective Essays on Guiding Deliberate Social Change.* San Francisco: Jossey-Bass, 1991.

Havel, V., *Politics as Morality in Practice: Speeches and Writings, 1990–1996.* New York: Knopf, 1997.

McLagan, P. & Nel, C., *The Age of Participation: New Governance for the Workplace and the World.* San Francisco: Berrett-Koehler, 1996.

Process-Oriented Psychology. Because we are living, we grow and change. Because we are aware, we notice similarities and differences—in other words, we notice changes. We also struggle to balance our identity with the need to change and adapt. Psychology is the discipline that studies these areas.

Process-Oriented Psychology is a holistic approach to understanding ourselves and our world. Its major spokesperson, Arnold Mindell, takes a very integrative approach to understanding human behavior. Process work unites physics, physiology, Jungian psychology, Gestalt psychology, Taoism, shamanism, and insights from most psychologies. It focuses on awareness and the importance of hearing all the signals in the body, in one's own psychology, in relationships, in groups, and in the world. Process work is currently being used to facilitate change and conflict resolution in organizations and communities throughout the world. It is also a fast-breakthrough approach to individual and relationship therapy.

For further insights, read:

Mindell, Amy, *Metaskills.* Tempe: New Falcon Publications, 1995.

Mindell, Arnold, *The Leader As Martial Artist: An Introduction to Deep Democracy.* San Francisco: Harper, 1992.

Mindell, Arnold, *Sitting in the Fire: Large Group Transformation Using Conflict and Diversity.* Portland: Lao Tse Press, 1995.

Index

action, 1, 15, 19–20, 23, 26, 29,
    37, 40, 43, 45, 56–57, 60, 61,
    64–65, 66, 71, 75–77, 78,
    81, 84, 87, 89, 90, 92, 95, 96,
    98, 100, 101, 102, 103,
    104–106, 108, 111, 112,
    114, 116–117, 119,
    121–122, 124–126,
    131–132, 135
  powerful, 1, 64, 87, 90, 92, 96,
    98, 100, 102, 104, 106,
    108, 112, 114, 116, 119,
    121-122, 124, 135
active, 35–36, 39, 41, 49, 102,
    108, 122, 135
  learning, 41, 102, 108, 122,
    135
alignment, 30–31, 34
appreciation, 76–77
assumptions, 57, 63–67, 71, 79,
    84, 98, 132, 135
belief
  awareness, 15, 17, 20, 21, 23,
    40, 57, 63–65, 67, 79, 81,
    84, 91, 95, 112, 119, 129,
    131, 133, 135

history of, 6, 32, 135
  powerful, 1, 5, 10, 14, 16, 18,
    20, 22, 26, 28, 30, 32, 34,
    36, 40, 42, 46, 48, 52, 54,
    56
breakthrough, 17, 22, 26–27, 69,
    99
business, 2, 6, 10, 17–19, 23, 33,
    35, 37, 43, 47, 58, 61, 78, 87,
    89–93, 96, 99, 101, 106,
    111, 119, 121–123,
    125–126, 130–132,
    135–136, 138, 140, 142
  basics, 99–100, 122
  capacity, 1, 31, 77, 99, 113, 131
change
  deliberate, 23, 25, 27, 40, 54,
    132, 135–136
  starts, 14, 19–23, 40, 46, 51,
    54, 107, 136
character, 1, 7, 57–60, 63–64, 66,
    69–70, 72, 75–76, 78–81,
    83–84, 87, 125–126, 135
  powerful, 1, 7, 56-57, 60, 64,
    66, 70, 72, 76, 78, 80, 84,
    135

commitment, 17, 19, 29–32,
    35–37, 40, 45–46, 48, 49,
    52, 54, 69, 115, 81, 91, 123,
    136
communication, 23, 30, 34, 63,
    64, 96–97, 100, 107, 119,
    132, 141
community, 10, 23, 39–40, 58,
    71, 95, 132
competencies, 91, 93, 96, 100,
    102–107, 121, 135
  worth, 20, 22, 84, 89, 99, 102,
    105–106, 122, 135
comply, 14, 111–112
conflict, 61, 69, 95–96, 133
consciousness, 40, 70, 79, 98,
    108–109, 117
control, 2, 6, 16–17, 27, 34, 45,
    53, 57, 71, 96, 114, 119,
    130
create, 6, 9, 14, 18, 25, 32, 39,
    45–46, 48, 51, 65, 69,
    90–91, 97–98, 103, 108,
    109, 114, 122, 132
critical thinking, 98, 122
decisions, 3, 35, 61, 67, 71, 84, 97,
    101, 108, 111, 122
deliberate change, 23, 25, 27, 40,
    54, 132, 135–136
deliver, 30, 89–90, 92, 102, 121
doers, 39
emotions, 13–17, 34, 40, 42,
    53–54, 57, 67, 69, 71–73,
    79, 81, 84, 98, 112, 123,
    135–136
  negative, 13–17, 26, 40, 42, 54,
    64, 66, 71, 77–79, 98,
    106, 135–136

positive, 6, 15, 66, 71–72,
    76–79, 85, 98, 106
empower, 11, 109, 132
  actions, 1, 19–20, 26, 37, 40,
    43, 45, 56–57, 61, 64–65,
    71, 75–77, 81, 87, 90, 92,
    96, 98, 100, 102,
    104–106, 108, 112, 114,
    116–117, 119, 121–122,
    124–126, 135
  character, 1, 7, 57–60, 63–64,
    66, 69–70, 72, 75–76,
    78–81, 83–84, 87,
    125–126, 135
evaluating, 41
feedback, 71, 76–78, 90, 92, 104,
    109, 121
financial, 96, 99–100, 108, 119,
    122, 141
followers, 39, 41–43, 46, 52, 54,
    136
formal leaders, 33, 35–37, 39, 48,
    54, 136
future, 1, 6, 13–16, 18, 21–22,
    27, 31, 35, 42–43, 49, 51,
    55, 72, 75, 77–79, 89,
    91–93, 97–98, 102,
    105–108, 112, 121–122,
    126, 129–130, 135
goals, 25, 28, 48, 90, 92–93,
    101–103, 109, 121, 135
grief cycle, 112–113
growth, 42, 73, 83, 108
hero, 113–117, 129
heroine, 113–117, 129
human resource, 30, 87, 101, 103,
    105, 107–109, 119, 122,
    135, 141

manager, 87, 101, 103, 105,
    107, 109, 119, 122, 135
information age, 65, 87, 95–100,
    117, 119, 122–123, 135
initiators, 125
innovation, 6, 40, 43, 48, 69, 96,
    104
intentions, 25, 64, 66
interpersonal, 95, 103
journey
    hero, 113–117, 129
    heroine, 113–115, 117, 129
    mainstream, 13, 19–20, 27, 34,
        115–117, 129
    marginalized, 115–117, 129
leadership, 29, 31–37, 39, 42–43,
    45–46, 48–49, 52, 54, 59,
    61, 69, 101, 105, 116,
    130–132, 136, 141, 142
learning, 11, 21, 25, 27–28,
    34–35, 37, 40–41, 48, 49,
    61, 64, 69–72, 77, 90–91,
    96–100, 102, 107–109, 112,
    114–115, 119, 122, 129,
    131–132, 135
listening, 41
mainstream, 13, 19–20, 27, 34,
    115–117, 129
management
    conflict, 61, 69, 95–96, 133
    human resource, 30, 87, 101,
        103, 105, 107–109, 119,
        122, 135, 141
marginalized, 115–117, 129
motivated, 91, 102–104, 107, 112,
    135
nature, 6, 14, 27, 31–32, 75, 77,
    95, 108, 111, 129–130

network, 23, 58, 90, 92, 102, 107,
    121–122, 135
normal, 9–11, 13, 20, 34, 40, 46,
    51, 53, 106, 136
optimism, 28, 75–78
participate, 19, 40, 42, 75, 99,
    112, 117
passion, 60
perfection, 34–35, 37
performance, 6, 14, 17, 71–72,
    96, 102–104, 131–132, 135,
    141–142
persistence, 13, 17
power, 1, 2, 5, 7, 10, 13, 14,
    16–18, 19, 20, 22, 26, 28, 29,
    30, 31, 32, 34, 35–36, 39, 40,
    41, 42–43, 45–46, 48, 52,
    54, 56–58, 60, 64, 66,
    69–70, 72, 76, 77, 78, 80, 84,
    87, 90, 92, 96, 98, 100–102,
    104–108, 109, 112–116,
    119, 121–124, 125, 130,
    132, 135
problem solving, 6, 97
purpose, 7, 9, 22, 56, 59–60, 77,
    107
questionnaires, 2
    empowered beliefs, 47–49
    empowered character, 83–85
    empowered actions, 121–123
reactions, 14, 21, 41–43, 66, 71,
    111–112, 125
relationships, 13, 34, 65, 96, 107,
    122, 131, 133
resist, 13–18, 20, 26–27, 34, 37,
    40, 42, 46–48, 51, 53–54,
    64, 69–72, 105, 112, 125,
    132, 135–136

resources
  continued learning, 129, 135
responsibility, 39, 41–42, 49, 57,
    66–67, 71, 72, 84, 101, 105,
    109, 125
risks, 11, 14, 16, 40, 42, 45
science, 6, 9, 66, 75–76, 130–132
self–management, 17, 103
skills, 3, 6, 17, 20, 23, 27, 34–35,
    53, 57, 72, 87, 91, 95–100,
    102–103, 105–108, 116,
    119, 121–123, 135
  information age, 65, 87,
      95–97, 99–100, 117, 119,
      122–123, 135
stability, 6, 9–10, 13, 34, 46, 51,
    53, 57, 61, 71, 114
strategy, 25, 28, 40, 43, 53, 69, 91,
    142
systemic, 96–98, 122

teaching, 96, 99–100, 119, 122
thinking
  creative, 69, 97–98, 108, 114,
      122, 132
  critically, 6, 36, 48, 79, 96–98,
      98, 122
  systemic, 96–98, 122
truth, 31, 42, 49, 63, 98, 106
value, 9, 13, 27, 29, 39, 57, 67, 75,
    77, 79, 81, 83–85, 89–90,
    97–98, 101–107, 135
vision
  future, 1, 6, 13–16, 18, 21–22,
      27, 31, 35, 42–43, 49, 51,
      55, 72, 75, 77–79, 89,
      91–93, 97–98, 102,
      105–108, 112, 121–122,
      126, 129–130, 135

About the Author

Pat McLagan has worked with organizations and people in change for over 30 years. She worked with Vietnam War vets to assist their shift to a university environment. She consulted with NASA to support the culture transition from moon shots to shuttle and space station; with GE on many major change projects to optimize results, people, and technology; with organizations and people in South Africa before, during, and after the end of apartheid.

She has also worked extensively in technology, financial services government, and many other areas to help organizations adapt to and influence rapid changes and relocations. In all this, her first love is supporting individuals at all levels, in all roles, to take charge of our lives and influence the changes around us.

Pat is the 15th person and second woman inducted into the Human Resource Development Hall of Fame, and is a member of the International Adult and Continuing Education Hall of Fame. She has received many leadership awards, including the highest award of the American Society for Training and Development—the Gordon M. Bliss Memorial Award.

She is a frequent conference keynote speaker and is Professor of Human Resource Management at Rand Afrikaans University in South Africa. She is co-author of *The Age of Participation: New Governance for the Workplace and the World,* and *On the Level: Performance Communication that Works,* plus numerous articles, studies and reports. She is CEO of McLagan International, Inc., a consulting and training company focused on implementing change and transforming the workplace.

She lives in Washington D.C. and Cape Town South Africa, and consults and works globally.

Find her at patmclagan@mclaganinternational.com

About McLagan International, Inc.

McLagan International, Inc. is a Washington, D.C. based company that provides services, products, and a consortium of highly experienced consultants to guide implementing and sustaining change.

Speeches   Executive Coaching   Consulting

- Change evaluations, business cases, and surveys
- Change Strategy and Strategy Implementation Planning support
- Performance Management as strategy implementation
- Workshops and support materials for leaders, change agents, employees at large
- theRITEstuff Reports, including *Success with Change:* THE ultimate best practice reports, drawing from the world's research into practices that get results.

Contact www.questions@mclaganinternational.com
Contact her at patmclagan@mclaganinternational.com

Berrett-Koehler Publishers

BERRETT-KOEHLER is an independent publisher of books, periodicals, and other publications at the leading edge of new thinking and innovative practice on work, business, management, leadership, stewardship, career development, human resources, entrepreneurship, and global sustainability.

Since the company's founding in 1992, we have been committed to supporting the movement toward a more enlightened world of work by publishing books, periodicals, and other publications that help us to integrate our values with our work and work lives, and to create more humane and effective organizations.

We have chosen to focus on the areas of work, business, and organizations, because these are central elements in many people's lives today. Furthermore, the work world is going through tumultuous changes, from the decline of job security to the rise of new structures for organizing people and work. We believe that change is needed at all levels—individual, organizational, community, and global—and our publications address each of these levels.

We seek to create new lenses for understanding organizations, to legitimize topics that people care deeply about but that current business orthodoxy censors or considers secondary to bottom-line concerns, and to uncover new meaning, means, and ends for our work and work lives.

See next pages for other publications from Berrett-Koehler

Corporate Creativity
How Innovation and Improvement Actually Happen

Alan G. Robinson and Sam Stern

Robinson and Stern have investigated hundreds of creative acts in organizations around the world to find the truth about how innovation and improvement really happen. They identify six essential elements that companies can use to turn their creativity from a hit-or-miss proposition into something they can count on.

Paperback, 300 pages • ISBN 1-57675-049-3
Item #50493-415 $17.95

Audiotape, 2 cassettes/3 hrs. • ISBN 1-56511-264-4
Item #12644-415 $16.95

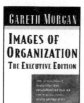

Images of Organization
—The Executive Edition

Gareth Morgan

Recognized as one of the most influential management texts of the last decade, *Images of Organization* revolutionized the way we look at organizations. Now this classic book has been revised to meet the needs of today's managers.

Hardcover, 400 pages • ISBN 1-57675-038-8
Item #50388-415 $35.00

Imaginization
New Mindsets for Seeing, Organizing, and Managing

Gareth Morgan

"Imaginization" is a key managerial skill that will help you develop your creative potential and find innovative solutions to difficult problems. *Imaginization* shows how to put this approach into practice.

Paperback, 350 pages • ISBN 1-57675-026-4
Item #50264-415 $19.95

Berrett-Koehler Publishers
PO Box 565, Williston, VT 05495-9900
Call toll-free! **800-929-2929** 7 am-9 pm EST

Or fax your order to 802-864-7627
For fastest service order online: **www.bkconnection.com**

Berrett-Koehler books and audios are available at quantity discounts for orders of 10 or more copies.

Change Is Everybody's Business

Pat McLagan

Paperback, 140 pages
ISBN 1-57675-190-2
Item #51902-415 $16.95

Special discounts for bulk purchases:

10-99	.25%	($12.71 each)
100-249	.30%	($11.87 each)
250-999	.35%	($11.02 each)
1,000-4,999	.40%	($10.17 each)
5,000-9,999	.50%	($8.48 each)

Ordering information

To order, please call us toll-free at 1-800-929-2929, fax us at **(802) 864-7626**, or email us at **bkp.orders@AIDCT.com**

To find out about our discount programs for resellers, please contact our Special Sales department at **(415) 288-0260**; Fax: **(415) 362-2512**. Or email us at **bkpub@bkpub.com**